Chronicles of the Coe Colony

Chronicles of the Coe Colony

Pea Ridge, Kentucky

Samuel S. Coe
with R. A. Adams

Edited with an Introduction by
Billy N. Guffey

Burkesville, Kentucky

Copyright 1930 by
Samuel S. Coe and R.A. Adams
Kansas City, Kansas

ISBN: 978-0-9797713-1-6
Library of Congress Control Number: 2007932549

First Xerxes Publishing Edition, 2007

Subjects: Coe Family
               African Americans - Kentucky

Published by Xerxes Publishing
P.O. Box 785
Burkesville, KY 42717
www.xerxespublishing.com

All additions to this work Copyright 2007 by Billy N. Guffey. All rights reserved. Printed in the United States of America. No part of the additional material may be used or reproduced in any manner whatsoever without written consent except in the case of brief quotations in articles and reviews. For information contact Xerxes Publishing, 412 Public Square, P.O. Box 785, Burkesville, KY 42717. E-mail: info@xerxespublishing.com.

On the cover: (L) Calvin Coe and (R) Thomas E. Coe, courtesy of Mr. and Mrs. Roger Tooley and Mrs. Brookie Stalcup, respectively.

Acknowledgements

Thanks are due to many people for the reprinting of this book, not the least of which is my family who have stood by and waited patiently for this project to be completed. Thanks also to Katrina Graves for typesetting in a very timely manner; to Dr. Lynwood Montell for his encouragement; and to Mr. and Mrs. Roger Tooley for their friendliness, their sharing of stories, and the use of the photograph of Calvin Coe on the cover of this book.

Contents

INTRODUCTION 11

CHAPTER 1 — GENEALOGIES AND MYSTERIES 15

CHAPTER 2 — A FUGITIVE SLAVE 21

CHAPTER 3 — CHRONICLES OF EZEKIEL COE 25

CHAPTER 4 — BILL COE AND HIS EXPLOITS 35

CHAPTER 5 — BEGINNING OF RACIAL STRIFE 43

CHAPTER 6 — "DARK AND BLOODY GROUND" 53

CHAPTER 7 — WHEN JUSTICE WAS NOT BLIND 61

CHAPTER 8 — A TRAIN OF EVENTS 69

CHAPTER 9 — THE GRIM REAPER REAPS 75

CHAPTER 10 — THE WAR BREAKS OUT ANEW 83

CHAPTER 11 — "THE YOUNGER GENERATION" 91

CHAPTER 12 — HIGH LIGHTS AND DEEP SHADOWS 101

CHAPTER 13 — REAPING THE WHIRLWIND 111

CHAPTER 14 — A MOTHER'S BROKEN HEART 115

CHAPTER 15 — TRANSGRESSIONS AND TRAGEDIES 121

CHAPTER 16 — AND THE STORY ENDS 137

ADDENDA

ADDENDA I — RUMINATIONS OF SAMUEL COE 147

ADDENDA II — PROHIBITION 150

ADDENDA III - PART 1 — TRUTH-SPIRIT-LOVE 155

ADDENDA III - PART 2 — SPIRIT 158

ADDENDA III - PART 3 — FAITH 160

ADDENDA III - PART 4 — LOVE   164

ADDENDA III — SUMMARY   166

ADDENDA IV - PART 1 — PARTY OR POLICY   167

ADDENDA IV - PART 2 — THE QUESTION OF IMPROVEMENTS   169

ADDENDA IV - PART 3 — A WARNING TO THE FARMER   170

ADDENDA IV - PART 4 — LAW ENFORCEMENT   171

ADDENDA IV - PART 5 — CRIME   173

ADDENDA V — RACE VARIETIES AND ANTAGONISMS   181

ADDENDA V - PART 1 — THE RECORD   182

ADDENDA V - PART 2 — ANTAGONISMS   189

ADDENDA V - PART 3 — WHAT IS IN A NAME   192

ADDENDA VI — COROLLARY   195

Introduction

There is not much information to be found regarding this book, "Chronicles of the Coe Colony," and its printing history. It is known that Samuel Coe is listed as the author along with R.A. Adams. This information is available from the Library of Congress, along with the fact that the book was published in Kansas City, Kansas in 1930.

The questions remain as to who these men were, and what part each played in the composition of the original manuscript.

We know that Samuel Coe was a son of Bill and Mandy Coe, and the grandson of Ezekiel and Patsy Ann Coe, the original settlers of the Coe Ridge Colony. It is thought that Samuel was born in 1879, which is corroborated in the book; for, in Chapter Ten the story is told of George Taylor's death at the "voting-place" in 1892, and later in the same chapter mentions "the writer, a boy of thirteen years." It is believed that he moved to Kansas City, Kansas when he was in his early twenties, around the turn of the century, although in this book it states, "In this very city of Indianapolis, in 1902, the writer was attacked by what is known as a bungelow gang." So the exact year Coe moved to Kansas City cannot be stated with certainty. It is generally thought that Samuel worked as a fireman in Kansas City and was also assisted with this book by members of the fire department with which he worked. He died in Kansas City in 1962.

R.A. Adams is believed to have been a white man that assisted Samuel Coe in writing his story. Information from the Library of Congress finds Adams referred to as a "joint author" for this book.

There is another listing by R.A. Adams in the LOC catalog which states that his full name was Revels Alcorn Adams, born in 1869, with a book titled, "The Social Dance" which was published in

Kansas City, Kansas circa 1921.

The description attached to the catalog listing for that book states, "This anti-dance treatise is divided into four parts. The first part discusses the physical effects of the dance, and the author concludes that habitual dancers are sick more often and that women are more prone to "female weaknesses." The second section focuses on the dangers of dance on the mind and concludes that many girls fail in school because they dance too much. In the third section, the author argues that dance is immoral and "fires the passions of young women." The concluding section is devoted to detailing passages in the Scriptures that the author interprets as supporting his arguments."

Information is scarce regarding Mr. Adams, and there is no actual proof that the two Adams' mentioned were actually the same person. There might have been more than one author named R.A. Adams, but the evidence does support that they were in fact one in the same. Besides the name, both books were published in Kansas City, Kansas; with a publishing year difference of approximately nine years. But the most convincing evidence is probably the fact that "Chronicles" ends with a section devoted to Scripture that supports his views throughout the book, which is strikingly similar to the description of the anti-dance treatise mentioned above.

"Chronicles of the Coe Colony" can be located in just a handful of libraries in the United States, and it seems that most are actually photocopies of the original book. The copy that was used for the purpose of transcription for this reprint is assumed to be consistent with other photocopies available, with some deciphering involved, as some text near the gutter was either smudged by the copying process, or so light in ink that it became unreadable. For that reason some small blanks had to be filled for the purpose of the story. If a complete readable copy exists and mistakes are detected in this text, we welcome the submission of corrections for a later reprint.

The original author(s) used an overabundance of punctuation throughout the book, of which much has been corrected. Spelling has also been corrected for the most part, except in instances of regional speech. Proper nouns have been changed as to spelling, such as, Glasgow instead of Glascow; Livingston instead of Leavenston; and so forth.

It should also be noted that it appears that Mr. Coe dictated much of the book. There are places in the text that, when referring to African Americans, will read "they", such as a person not of that race might tend to write. As the Addenda at the rear of the book begins, the "writer", meaning Samuel Coe, is mentioned as not having been born during the slave period; and then the "scribe" is mentioned as having lived during this same slave period in Kansas City. So the supposition that the story was told by Coe to Adams, et al, seems to hold some weight.

This book is being brought to press for the first time in many decades for the purpose of making it available to those who have never had the pleasure of reading it. For these pages hold a history like none other. The people that inhabited Coe Ridge, from the beginning of the Colony until its ultimate demise, show us a family devoted not only to itself, but also to the basic principles of life, liberty and justice.

An excellent companion volume to this book is Dr. William Lynwood Montell's, *The Saga of Coe Ridge: A Study in Oral History*, which includes an early Coe family tree, and is considered one of the best sources of overall information regarding the Coe Colony of Pea Ridge, Kentucky.

Billy N. Guffey, 2007

CHAPTER ONE
GENEALOGIES AND MYSTERIES

A Story of the old,
And yet, one of the new;
As long as live the characters,
The story is not thru;
A story to be written down,
A story well worth while,
A story to make you lament,
And also, make you smile.

In Cumberland County, State of Kentucky, just across the Tennessee-Kentucky line, in the 18th Century, were born two girls of mysterious parentage and of dark complexion. Little is known of their ancestry, because they belonged to the period of black slavery in America when little was known and less cared concerning the parentage of a dark child or the identity of such a child. According to information considered reliable, the mother was dark and the father, who was unknown, was said to be an Indian. The older sister was called Betty, and the younger one, Sukey.

Being slaves, and like all other slaves, subject to their master in everything, these girls were used just as their master saw fit to use them, and under such conditions and circumstances they grew into womanhood and became mothers at an early age. Betty was the mother of two proud sons, named Ezekiel and nicknamed Zeek and Rance; Sukey gave birth to a son who was named Riley, and a daughter, named Patsy.

Whether the children of these two sisters were related on their father's side or not is not known, but they belonged to the same master and lived and worked in the same place and under the same conditions. In the case of the girl and the boy, children of the younger sister, the boy must have been the son of some white man, because I can remember he was spoken of as being very "bright".

It is scarcely possible that the readers should be familiar with the attitude of white men of that period in regard to illegitimate children born to slave women, hence it might be well to explain that, if the mixed-breed slave child was too bright, they would "South him"; that is, they would sell him to slave traders who would take him into the worst section of the South. This is what happened to Riley. Having in his veins the blood of three races, the dominant whites, the royal Croutau, and the unconquerable Indian, and the combined peculiarities of them all, he was difficult to understand and to get along with.

For the reason just given, Riley's master, Jack Coe, decided to sell him to the "slave traders," with the expectation that they would take him to the far South, where he would serve under overseers and hard task-masters. So this boy, with the strange blood-mixture, went to the block, was sold to the highest bidder, and was carried far away to the real South, from which it was thought he would never return. But, as in many cases, the plans miscarried, as the sequel will show.

This boy, Riley, or man as he was then, was of such temperament and such courage, and was so proud and manly, that he resolved never to take cruel punishment from any man, and if he should be forced to do so, he would take vengeance on the man who would mistreat him. Because of mistreatment he became dissatisfied in the South, into which they had sold him, and where he was forced to work on cotton plantations and cane fields; so he ran off, and made his way back to his master's house. But according to the law, being the property of his new master, he could not remain in his old home, in Kentucky.

It was the custom in slave states, when Croutau people desired to marry, that the master approve, and he performed the ceremony. The master would hold the broomstick, order the bride and groom to jump over; and when they had done this he pronounced them man and wife. So Zeek, the son of Betty, and Patsy, the daughter of Sukey, jumped over the broomstick together, by which Zeek became the brother-in-law of Riley and the son-in-law of Sukey. And according to prevailing customs they became members of the same family.

One day about nine months after Riley had been sold, while Zeek and his master were walking near Kettle Creek, in Cumberland County, near the Tennessee line, Zeek discovered familiar footprints which he recognized as those of his brother-in-law, Riley, and, for fear, he refrained from calling his master's attention to what he had discovered. Returning to the cabin in which he lived, he found Riley there and heard the story of his abuse in the far South, and of his escape; and, regardless of consequences pledged him his aid and protection.

All who know of the conditions prevailing during the time of slavery know of the attitude of a slave owner when he had lost his investment in slave property. Well, Riley had been sold for sixteen hundred dollars ($1,600); had escaped, and therefore represented that much loss to his new owner. But, the owner did not concede the loss, considering the slave was still his property, as long as he was alive. Every effort was used to capture the fugitive slave; they used detective agencies and blood hounds, and searched from the line of Kentucky to the Gulf of Mexico; but they failed utterly in all their efforts. In the meanwhile, the slave for whom they were seeking was being safely concealed among his relatives and friends.

The slave-hunters were instructed that they must find the fugitive if he remained on the earth; so they continued with great diligence, for twelve months longer with the same fruitless result. On one occasion, the slave-trader talked with Riley's mother, and she reminded him that her son was light enough to pass for one of them, so that he could escape detection, and hinted that perhaps he had gone to other parts, changed his name, and thus it might be possible that the owner would never recover his loss. This caused the white man to consider some other plan by which he might save himself from total loss. It was then that he began to think of a possible deal with his former master, to that effect.

One day Jack Coe heard a familiar voice, calling "Hallo, Jack Coe!" Then the question, "Do you know anything about the slave you sold me?" Continuing, "He ran away and we can't find him. I came to ask if you know whether he is alive, and to make a proposition to you, that you will buy him back, if he is alive, so that money paid to you for him will not be all lost." "But I am not responsible," Mr. Coe answered sharply, adding, "I, I do not know where he is, if he is alive." "But I want to know if you will buy him back and take your chances," insisted the trader. Jack Coe looked down for a brief period, then, lifting his head said, "Tho it is only taking a chance, since I don't know whether he is dead or alive, but I will give you five hundred dollars ($500.00) and take chances on finding him."

This was of course an interesting proposition for the former owner of the slave. He had sold him for sixteen hundred dollars ($1,600), and if he could buy him back for the small sum of $500.00, his profit would be great. While the trader was considering the proposition, he decided to talk it over with Zeek, who, tho a slave, had the confidence of his master and often advised him in matters of considerable importance. Moreover, other slaves confided in him, as well as did his master.

Now Zeek was a small man, weighing only one hundred fifteen pounds, but this little light colored, grey-eyed, brown-haired man was sharp in mind. He was a reader of men and very seldom missed in his judgment concerning anything. Following his usual custom of reading men, Zeek listened very attentively as his master talked concerning Riley and the proposition to have him buy him, and take the chance of finding him. He looked the white man in the eye, studied him with a great diligence, and tried to decide whether he trusted him or not. He wanted the good will of his master; he wanted to keep his confidence; yet, he considered that he must protect his friend and kinsman. Studying his master he was inclined to trust him. It had been a terrible strain to keep a man hidden in his house for eighteen months. He had been watched, questioned, tantalized, and even tortured; he wanted relief from the great strain; but he was not willing to reveal the secret if it would make vain all that he had suffered; so Zeek was greatly puzzled.

About convinced he could trust his master and being anxious to do what was best, looking him steadily in the eyes he said, "Master, you have been very kind to your slaves; I have found you to be a good and truthful man, and I ought to be willing to trust you" — But, before he could finish, Jack Coe said with great earnestness, "You can trust me, and if you can find Riley, I have the five hundred dollars ready to pay for him, and he can remain here, on the plantation with us as before." Zeek heaved a sigh of relief and said, "If you mean all you have said, I will try to find the fugitive in a month or two." Jack Coe accepted Zeek's word and the discussion ended, for that time.

Of course it was no trouble for Zeek to find his brother-in-law, who had been hidden in his house during the entire eighteen months which they searched for him, but, for reasons of his own, he said he would try to find him, and specified "in a month or two," because he did not want it suspected that he was there. So, on the word of his slave, Jack Coe closed the contract, paid the five hundred dollars and bought back the slave which he had sold and sent into the South. He was confident that he was alive and that Zeek would find him.

Late one afternoon Riley was found in a little patch of woods, about a mile from the house. He was smiling and whistling, as if nothing had ever gone wrong. There was great anxiety to know the secret of how this slave had been concealed there for eighteen months. Perhaps the story was never made public; so, now that the dark days of slavery are gone forever, and we live in a new era, and because now, at this distance, no harm can follow, I have undertaken to write, in full, this interesting story.

CHAPTER TWO
A FUGITIVE SLAVE

Little is known of the boyhood days of Riley, the slave, but one prominent feature of his childhood and early manhood was that there was no trouble between him and his master. Jack Coe, tho a slave owner, was a man of integrity, and was humane in dealing with his slaves. One unusual thing and one for which he deserves great credit, was that he would not separate husband and wife by selling either from the other; nor would he sell a baby from its mother's arms, nor the mother from her child. No matter what the circumstances, neither the love of money nor the desire for prosperity would induce him to resort to such inhuman cruelty. In this he was far better than the majority of slave owners who cared nothing for their slaves except the profit from their labor.

Jack Coe had no grievance against Riley, but the fact was that shortly after his sister, Patsy and Zeek jumped over the broom-stick, their children began to come, making them more profitable to their master than was bachelor Riley. So when the time came that someone must be sold the lot fell on Riley, and he, the less profitable one was sold, while the others remained.

Shortly after the sale, Riley's new master put him on a horse and started with him to the far-off South, to his own sorrow and the grief of his mother and other relatives left behind. It required four days to make the long, tiresome journey. Arriving there, the boy who had been reared without abuse found the tasks assigned very heavy and the treatment far different from that of his generous master; and, under the circumstances there came to him the temptation to run away and return home to his old master and his kinfolk. He thought of his home and his loved ones; he was disgusted with his treatment; and he decided that he would go home, no matter the cost. After secretly securing information concerning the way best to go, he braved the dangers and started on his way.

It was necessary that this slave should begin his journey around midnight, waiting until all were asleep, and making that early start, in order to cover as much of the distance before day would dawn. He well knew that when his escape would be known, the blood hounds and "patter-rollers" as the Croutaus called them would be right on his trail. Surely he made very rapid speed, for he was on his journey two days before his pursuers were near enough to alarm him. Under the necessity to save himself, his mind was very active and must have worked rapidly. At every fork of the road he would stop and consider carefully which road to take; and, almost invariably he would take the right road.

As this fugitive told afterward, he was forced to crawl into a hollow log where he was certain there were snakes, making the action very dangerous; but he feared the poisonous reptiles in the log less than he did those inhuman forms who were pursuing him, and who, perhaps would have killed him. Lying there, exposed to such danger, he heard his pursuers pass by. After waiting quite a while, to be sure they had gone, he creeped out and began again his journey.

PEA RIDGE, KENTUCKY

After a long and perilous journey, this runaway slave reached the home from which he had been carried and the cabin of his mother. He traveled by night and kept in hiding by day, and during the last three days had neither food nor water, and in this condition he was when he arrived at his mother's cabin. Her heart was full of joy, because she had given up hope of ever seeing him again. Before his mother could make an outcry, he put his finger on his lips as a signal for her to be quiet. Drawing near to her he whispered, "I ran away; I have had nothing to eat or drink for three days; I am hungry, tired and weary; do your will, bring me something to eat and drink, out to the barn where I must hide."

Perhaps no one but a mother could understand the feelings of that mother as she hurried around the kitchen preparing food for her son, and as she thought of him as having been three days without food. Well, soon she had all things ready and carried the food to the barn. Riley recognized her footsteps, came out to the door of the barn to meet her; but he cautioned her to get away quickly and to be very careful, because the pursuers knew he was on his way home and would soon be there searching for him. They were soon there, too, but failed to find any trace of him. But, in anger the owner said, "I'll have that slave if he stays on top of the earth" — but he did not remain "on top of the earth," and the man-hunt was without avail.

Members of the family held a council to decide what was best to do, and how best to protect Riley. Some thought best that he should try to make his way to Canada. Another suggestion was to keep him hidden in the house.

It was finally decided to keep him there and try to save him, tho they knew the risk they were running. The cabin in which Zeek lived had a small cellar and it was agreed they would dig it out to make it deeper and larger and keep him in it. When they were discussing it someone asked, "But what can we do with the dirt?" The answer was, "Wait till it rains."

The scheme worked well; the work of digging went on; on rainy days, sometimes while the master was right there in the cabin, the Croutau was working, and digging out the sub-basement for his hiding place. They would carry the dirt to the creek, while it was raining, and so the fresh dirt was always washed away, leaving no trace to betray them. The under-ground home was finished and in it Riley lived during those eighteen months while they were searching for him almost everywhere.

CHAPTER THREE
CHRONICLES OF EZEKIEL COE

As was true of slaves in general, little is known of the early life of Ezekiel. It might be summarized; "He was born sometime during the year 1815; was a slave, the property of Jack Coe; was a good, obedient slave, was liked by his master, had his confidence, and was shown kindness and consideration unusual for slaves. But there was one thing to which he could not become reconciled, and that was to being punished as he saw other slaves punished." The following incidents will illustrate the confidence of Jack Coe in his Croutau slave, Zeek.

During the early years of his life, frequently he made the trip with his master to New Orleans to sell his produce. These trips were made on a flatboat. As a general thing the master demanded his money in gold and silver, which of course was heavy. This money was carried in a bag, and the carrying of the bag was entrusted to Zeek, and tho they often traveled good distances on foot, and the slave would get tired, he never complained of his burden.

Zeek and his master were returning from one of these trips on a steamboat, and there was on the boat, also, a professional wrestler, and Jack Coe said to the manager, "I bet you a hundred dollars that my slave can throw your man." The manager asked, "Has he had any training?" His master replied, "No, but I have confidence in him and am willing to put up the money." The manager asked to see this wonderful slave. Having seen him he laughed Jack Coe to scorn, saying, "Why that little fellow would do well to wrestle with a rooster, but he would be no match for my man; why he would put his head thru the bottom of the boat." "Well," he continued, "if you are willing to take the chance, I'll let the champion take a whip out of him, and I'll carry off your hundred dollars and make you the laughing stock of the country." Laughing, Jack Coe said, "Wal, if your man can do all that I'm willing to lose my money."

So, the champion came and they entered the ring marked off on the deck of the boat, and the contest was on. There was great excitement, and for a while it looked as if the champion would win. It was about decided the master had played the fool and lost his money. When the contest was so close and amid excitement, the master would call out, "Throw him Zeek, by zounds!" It seemed that when he heard his master's voice calling to him Ezekiel gained courage and strength. He made a great struggle; put forth his greatest strength, and finally pinned the champion's shoulders to the mat, won the match and saved his master's money.

Back in 1840, before machinery was very much in use, and when it was scarcely known back in the hills of Kentucky, Ezekiel learned basket-making, the trade of his times. Baskets and other articles were made and chairs were re-bottomed with bark of hickory trees. In the springtime Zeek would go out into the woods and, with his hatchet and drawing-knife gather enough bark for a year's work. Being so much in favor with his master, he had opportunity superior to those of other slaves. So, he would do his regular tasks and then it was his custom to work late at nights and on holidays to make money for himself.

After he was married to Patsy Ann, he began to work, even harder than before, and to save more money. Tho he kept it a secret, it was his hope and his intention to save money and buy himself and his wife from their master, in order that both of them might be free. Patsy Ann was a faithful woman, a loving companion, and a kind mother, and he was as anxious concerning her as he was concerning himself, and for this reason he was more industrious than he might have been otherwise. To Zeek and Patsy were born fourteen children, and from them sprang what were known as "The Coe boys, of Pea Ridge, Kentucky," a little scope of country bound on the north by Judio Creek, on the east by Kettle Creek, and on the south and west by the Cumberland River.

The Civil War period was a serious time for both master and slave. The North was fighting to save the Union; the South to hold its slaves; and the slaves dreamed of and prayed for freedom. Yet, with the slaves sad was the thought of leaving their masters who had been kind to them. All these emotions were experienced by Zeek and his family in common with other slaves who had humane masters. Finally the Civil War was over; peace was declared; all slaves were free; and, this man and his family, with millions of others, were happy to see the sun rise on a land of peace, and a land from which slavery had been banished forever.

Being free, Ezekiel Coe now realized that he and his family must plan and provide for themselves, even to the extent of leaving their master's plantation, where they had lived for so long; and the thought of it brought sadness to them, since he had been so kind to them, and there had been much friendly relationship between the slaves and their master. But they knew the day of freedom was the day for which they had longed and prayed. Zeek knew that thru the long dark days he had prayed to live to see the day when his children and his grand-children would be free from the encumbrance of slavery. He had looked forward to the happy time when in his efforts to be a man, he could provide and care for his family as he desired. To this end he had saved his money, and, when freedom came, he took his family and moved to Pea Ridge, the place previously mentioned. They settled, as bees in a hive, and tried to make good, but, alas, the struggle was more than had been expected.

In moving to Pea Ridge, in 1866, Ezekiel took with him his wife, his own mother, his mother-in-law, and ten children, among them six boys who were under twenty-five years of age. All these young men were strong; as hearty as a mule, as agile as a cat, and as game as a lion. Being willing to meet any requirements, they were just the kind for the work to be done there, for the section into which they moved was little less than a wilderness. Ezekiel had bought, for the settlement of his tribe, three hundred acres of land having valuable timber, some of the trees measuring nine feet in diameter. However, not realizing the value of the land he suffered considerable loss in regard to the timber.

During the first three years of life in this new settlement, Zeek had some experiences from which he learned some very important lessons. Because of the honesty and the fairness of his master, Jack Coe, he concluded that all white men were of the same kind and would be fair in their dealings with him. However, after these experiences, he knew better, and perhaps he never did have the same confidence in white people as he had before.

This loss of confidence was for Zeek a serious matter and it was the precursor of distrust, misunderstandings, mistreatment, and antagonisms between white people and those who had been slaves. At that time, this man who had so fully trusted his fellows, who were more fortunately circumstanced, was rudely awakened to the fact that he could not depend on his more fortunate neighbors for honesty and fair dealings — and it was to him a shock and a surprise.

This spirit of unfairness and injustice on the part of the descendants of these who were unfair, and the consequent loss of confidence on the part of those who have been treacherously dealt with constitute the basis of nearly all the racial antagonism and racial strife which have persisted thru the years. And these have hindered the development of the spirit of amity and racial cooperation. Yes, these were sad experiences for old man Zeek.

The first of these serious experiences was when he entered into a contract with a white man in regard to cutting timber for him. According to the contract, Ezekiel was to cut down the trees on his own land, saw them into logs twelve to fourteen feet long, and in return this white man was to grant use of his teams to haul Zeek's logs to the market. In regard to this contract he had serious disappointment, for, when he had finished his part of the contract, and reported the same to this white man, he flatly refused to keep the contract, and his logs were left in the woods to rot. In spite of this disappointment that shook his confidence in the integrity of the white man, he did not stop. He still believed that there were some white men that were honest; that there must be, or there would not have been the thirteenth and fourteenth Amendments to the Constitution of the United States; and so he was determined to keep on trying to succeed, and to hold on to his faith.

This exceptional Croutau had no knowledge of books and knew nothing about figures, yet his mind was alert, and he thought out clearly what was best for himself and family and for their interests. He would not give up trying to be righteous, honest, and intelligent, trying in honesty to be the equal of any man, white, black, or Indian. He considered that he belonged to three races, since, as to blood he was 50% white, 25% colored and 25% Indian, and to be fair he must be honest in dealings with all. So, acting on this principle he endeavored to so live, no matter how others dealt with him.

This man, honest in his own heart, did not lose hope because one white man had deceived him, but was willing to believe others honest until they should prove otherwise. He realized that white people owned the country and executed the laws, and there was no where to go, where he would not be associated with white people and dealing with them. After another hard year's work by him and his sons they marketed timber that sold for more than a thousand dollars, and then he had another shock and another very sad disappointment.

The new disappointment was that the white man in paying him for the logs gave him a number of one dollar bills for one hundred dollar bills, and, being ignorant in these matters and unable to count money, he had to accept the white man's word. When he did realize his loss he decided to go to law and sue the man who had cheated him, but he failed to consider that the lawyer, the witnesses, the jurymen and the judge would all be white, and would be against him. He was beaten in court, was compelled to pay the cost, and returned home disappointed and broken in spirit. Under these circumstances he thought of his master, Jack Coe, and he was certain that if this man who had been so kind to him, had ever thought that he would have been treated that way, he would have permitted him to learn enough for his own protection, even tho the law did prohibit it. Then, he thought of the Civil War Amendments, and in a cheerful spirit, said, "I am so glad that my children and my grandchildren will have opportunity to learn and thus protect themselves against such treatment."

In 1869 three of the older children of Ezekiel Coe were married, bringing into the Pea Ridge Colony three strangers. Mary Coe was married to Thomas Wilburn, a robust, healthy, excitable fellow, who was willing to live in peace with everybody if allowed to do so. Thomas Coe took as his wife, Lucettie King, a young woman who had never been a slave. The white Kings who owned her parents set them free, even before the Civil War began. To this couple were born four children, but, unfortunately, the father died when they were quite young, leaving to the mother the task of bringing them up. Bill Coe married a young woman named Mandy Kirkpatrick, a fine, well-bred young woman who made him an excellent wife and bore him seven children. She belonged to some of the best people of the slavery period. She had good character, had been taught good manners and the art of weaving and knitting; and, tho the law prohibited it, she had been taught to read. In spite of these qualities and accomplishments, Mandy did not hesitate to go out into the field and plow corn, if necessary.

About the year 1879, with a number of young children in the Pea Ridge District, the Colony faced the problem of education for these children. There was no school building, and there were no teachers. The State had not provided funds for the education of children of the freedmen, because they could not pay any quota of taxes. Some of the less intelligent white people thought that because they could not pay taxes, as did the white people, they were not entitled to the benefits of public schools.

While it must be admitted that the burden of taxes rested largely upon the white people, who were the owners of the property, yet, if the dark children had been permitted to attend the same schools as the whites, there would have been no increase of taxes. Moreover, consideration should have been labored nearly two hundred and fifty years, for white people, and for the prosperity of the nation, receiving just food and clothes, and sometimes only a small supply of these. There was no ignoring of the fact that because of this service they were entitled to any possible assistance in preparing for citizenship and its problem.

Notwithstanding the justice of their demands and the injustice of those who refused them, the Croutau people of the Pea Ridge Colony came together to devise ways and means by which to meet this absolute necessity; and they decided to open a school for their own children, whatever the cost. Then, there came the next problem, for there were no Croutau persons among them competent to teach these children. Of course they had no knowledge of the requirements of schools, and of school work, but doing the best they knew, they elected a board of trustees and began their arrangements to have school for their children during the next year.

The white teachers refused to teach colored children, and it became necessary to look for teachers of their own race competent to teach. There was just one Croutau woman in the Colony that knew much more than the alphabet, and they were willing to have her teach the children as far as she knew, but she was timid and would not trust herself, and so the search continued. Finally, they found a white man who was about a third grade teacher, and who agreed to take charge of their school, with the understanding that they would supplement his salary out of their own pockets. This white man taught for them one or two years, and the school term was just three months of each year.

Time passed on, and every year, there were more children becoming of school age. And those who were being taught were advancing; therefore it became necessary to search still, for a competent teacher. In the year 1884, a man by name of Bill Raspberry came to the Colony. No one knew where he came from, but he was employed as a teacher. Not only did Raspberry give satisfaction as a teacher, but he rendered service in the community in various ways, and thus he won the respect, confidence and gratitude of the people.

This man Bill Raspberry married Bill Coe's eldest daughter, and, after having taught the public school for more than ten years, he moved, with his wife and children to Indianapolis, Indiana, where he lived for twenty-five years. After his children were all grown, he informed them that his right name was not Raspberry, but Essleman. And, without making any explanation, he advised them to take the name Essleman. Raspberry, or Essleman, died about 1916.

In 1888 there were three classes of white people in the Pea Ridge District. Those of the first class were well bred, agreeable, willing to live in peace and harmony, and trying to do justice to all classes. Next came those who were indifferent to the welfare of other people, but wanted everything for themselves. The third class was composed of those who cared little for themselves and little for other people. They were always doing something to make trouble, were ready to steal, and even to commit murder, if aroused.

To correctly analyze and describe the Coe boys at this time would be a difficult task, but this much can be said: they were kind, clever, agreeable, generous, and always ready to assist any needy person or needy cause; still they were very queer specimens of humanity. In dealing they had no respect for person or color, contending that color has nothing to do with making a man. They knew that only recently the nation had purged itself from slavery, and they must be forever on the lookout against those who were still inclined to disregard their rights and deprive them of their privileges.

In temperament these boys were not quick to anger, but, once aroused, they would defend themselves, using anything within their reach. Greatly provoked, they would do bodily injury, and even take life, if they must do so in defense of their rights and their own lives. They were industrious, their chief occupation being farming and hauling logs, but, in these they were not very successful. They were strictly honest, preferring to be cheated than to cheat another person. They were generous, usually willing to divide whatever they had with others who were in need. Perhaps this strict honesty and this excessive generosity are somewhat responsible for their lack of prosperity, and their failures in business transactions.

In 1879, there was a heated political campaign, and a Dr. Hunter was a candidate from the Pea Ridge District, for representative. The Coe boys knowing that they were free, and according to the constitution were entitled to rights as citizens, were determined to demand their rights and exercise their privileges, at all hazards and at whatever cost; and they were interested in this campaign.

Also interested in Dr. Hunter's campaign were two young white men, Wright Capps and George Taylor. Capps was not considered a bad fellow and never had been known to kill anybody nor seriously to injure anyone. He had an old-fashioned cap-and-ball revolver, that when it was fired would discharge two or three shells at one time.

Sometimes when he was drunk, he would discharge his gun and frighten the children, but the adults were not alarmed. But the man Taylor was a terror. He was brave; was not afraid of anybody or anything; and he was never known to show sympathy or cowardice, or hoist the white flag, till he met the Coes.

One night, these men, Capps and Taylor went to the Pea Ridge District, bent on mischief. They went first to Bill Coe's house, and, instead of calling "hallo" as was the custom, especially at night, they came right up to the door and one said in a harsh tone, "Hunter men!" One of the little boys misunderstood and thought the man said "murder men." And, so he ran and hid under the bed. Mandy, Bill Coe's wife, rushed to the door, drew up a table and pushed against the door to bar the way. Bill rushed to the door, saying, "Take care, Mandy," opened the door and invited the men to come in and have seats. George Taylor sat down, but Wright Capps remained standing.

The Taylor boys were known to be treacherous, and it was said of George, that when he was talking politics he would keep his head down and his eyes partly closed, perhaps to prevent identification, in case of trouble; and so he did, at this time. Without giving the reason for their visit these two men left Bill Coe's. Believing they intended mischief, Bill sent his two boys to warn his younger brother, and with instructions to send the word to his uncle Calvin, that these men were on the hill and no doubt were looking for him.

The word went rapidly, and the message was that they'd take no chances. So all the others were on the alert; they were watchful until late in the night, then, thinking the danger over they returned to their homes; and the remainder of the night was quiet. During the remainder of the campaign there was no serious trouble and everything went on quietly until the year 1888, when the serious trouble began in the Pea Ridge District.

CHAPTER FOUR
BILL COE AND HIS EXPLOITS

———◆◆✕◆◆———

Bill Coe was born in 1845, and lived with his old master until he was ten years old. From that time until the beginning of the Civil War, in 1861, he lived with a man named Sam Moore. Then, because his master thought the slaves would be free in Kentucky before they would in Texas, he concluded to send them to that state. They traveled some in wagons and others on horseback, and Bill was one that rode horseback, all of the way; and he told wonderful stories of what happened on the trip. As Bill tells it, he thought very seriously of deserting the company, running away and trying to make it to the Union Army. At one time, so he stated, he actually wheeled his horse around to make the start. But, lacking experience concerning the army and knowledge of the country through which he must go to reach the army, he changed his mind and went on with the others.

Another one of Bill's experiences was in Arkansas. As is related by Bill, they had pitched tents near a cane brake, and he was sent to get a bucket of water. He had to go thru the dense growth of canes to reach the spring. When he did get there, he dashed his bucket into the spring, and out jumped some kind of a large animal and sprang at him, at the same time, making a loud noise. And Bill laughed, afterward, and declared the folks in the west did not have to wait long for the water.

At one place, about four o'clock in the morning, the report of a gun was heard, and when the cause was explained, a man had been found in the attempt to steal one of the horses, and the master had fired at him and missed him. Bill said, afterward, he was glad the thief did not get the horse, yet he was glad the master missed him and saved having the stain of blood on his hands. There were many more of these exploits which it was Bill's custom to tell, for his was an eventful life. Finally, they reached Texas, with no serious loss, and in Texas, Bill had a new master, a man named Stephenson. Whom he served four years during the remainder of the period of the Civil War, until the war ended and the slaves were made free.

Bill Coe told many stories of his experiences during these four years spent in Texas. One was of a fight with his master's son; another was a wrestle with a strong woman who had been able to throw every man with whom she had contested; and one was an occasion on which he became so excited that he slapped two stones together in his master's face, and said, "If you try to hurt me, I'll fight you as quick as I'll fight any man!"

Interesting was Bill's story of how he saved his life when attacked by a furious bull. He was carrying a tanned hide, when he was met by a herd of cattle and this bull came running and charging furiously. With rare presence of mind, Bill stepped aside and threw the tanned hide across the back of the charging animal; this action saved him, because the bull became frightened and changed his course.

Another story was how Bill acted as peace-maker when two neighbors had an altercation. These neighbors were carrying their guns to kill each other but Bill succeeded in having them make peace.

There was told the story of one of Bill Coe's physical feats which was surprising. At a saw mill, some young men were trying to put a huge log on a carriage but could not succeed. Bill and his brother Tom observed the futile efforts, and the former asked, "Can I help you, boys?" And the foreman readily consented.

This modern Samson picked up the hook used to lift logs, clapped it around the log, and braced himself for the effort. His brother Tom called, "Look out, Bill, don't break that pole." The young men laughed! One sneered and said, "You can't do it when four or five of us couldn't." But Bill said, "If this pole don't break I'll put it on." But the pole broke and the splinters flew everywhere.

Laughing, Bill said, "Get me a handstick that won't break and I'll show you what I'll do." They gave him another stick; he squatted, raised up and the log tumbled over on the carriage; then Bill and Tom went on their way.

When peace was declared, the master told the slaves they were as free as he was, and they would have to look out for themselves. It was then that our hero, Bill Coe, with a number of others started back to Kentucky, riding in wagons and on horses, as they had gone into Texas. Bill tells some amusing and interesting incidents connected with this journey, also.

Perhaps the most interesting one of these experiences was the one in which he had a fight with a vicious dog. The wagon had stopped and Bill went to a house which was not far from the road, to get some water. As he was nearing the house a vicious dog ran to meet him. Now, this many-sided fellow having had experience with dogs, boasted that he had a way he could tame any dog and cause him to make friends with him. It was his scheme that when the dog would come near, he would just step aside and as the dog would pass him, he would put the hat on the dog's head. In such cases, he claimed, the dog not only would not bite him, but would make amends with him. So, when the dog came the first time, Bill snatched off his hat and clapped it on the dog's head. He ceased his attack, but would not make friends, and in a few minutes he was after Bill again. The second time he put his hat on the dog's head, but it failed as before. When the dog came the third time, he stepped aside, and just as the animal passed he kicked him in the ribs, as hard as could, and the dog went away howling with pain, but did not return to the attack.

A man who was the owner of the home, and of the dog, was standing near, all of the time, and when he was informed that Bill only wanted some water from his well, he permitted him to have it; but he could never understand why this man made no effort to restrain the dog when he was trying to bite him. Realizing that they were amid unfriendly surroundings, the travelers soon moved on their journey to Kentucky.

Returning to Kentucky, Bill made his way to the Pea Ridge District and to the home of his father, Ezekiel Coe. He tried as earnestly as he could to help make the colony worth while. The pole axe and the broad axe were his specialties, and he did not think there was any one there who could excel him in the use of his favorite tools. In cutting trees, hewing logs, making stock for the old single plow, building a house, sharpening and setting saws, Bill was a master, a man of many talents, and difficult to equal; but Bill's great strength proved his misfortune, in one way, it caused him to over-estimate it and exhaust it.

At one time, during the early days of the Colony, Bill again distinguished himself as a man of great strength. They were clearing new ground and had set apart a day for log-rolling, and Bill Coe was to be a prominent figure in the exercise.

It was reported that two white men had boasted that they could carry more logs than Bill and Tom, Bill's brother. Bill laughed and said, "I ain't trying to beat nobody, but this race will get more logs moved than any other way." So he and Tom accepted the challenge and the contest was on.

Bill and Tom would take the stick on one side of a log and the two white men on the other side, and, in that way, all thru the day, they carried many logs of different lengths and weights. They did not finish and it was agreed to return the next day and complete the work.

On the second day the work began with the same arrangements as on the previous one. In the afternoon it was noticed that one of the white men had begun to weaken, while Bill and Tom were at strong as ever and carrying their loads without faltering.

According to Bill's story, it was the custom to have at least a gallon of whiskey at a log-rolling. This they had on the first day, and Bill said when he'd drink whiskey he felt like he could move a mountain; so they drank the entire gallon on that first day and had to get another gallon for the second day.

Beginning as usual they would place their hand sticks under the log and walk away with it. At the time mentioned, when the word was given, this white man failed to raise his end of the stick. Bill laughed at him and said, "Move, all of you, and I'll carry it all by myself!" Nobody believed he could or even that he would try, but while they looked on in amazement, this giant raised one end of the log and carried it and dropped it on the wagon.

Another log story was that at one time something happened to the wagon on which some men were loading logs, and Bill held up the end of the log while they fixed the wagon. It was even told that he carried a log sixty feet long and eighteen inches in diameter.

A white man who saw Bill holding up the end of the log circulated the report that he had seen him holding up two trees at the same time. Another white man had said he was going to "whip ole Bill Coe" the first time he saw him; but he changed his mind after he heard the report about holding up the two trees.

At another time Bill had a fight with a white man. He declared, "I did not want to fight nobody, the white man made me do it." While in a field near the man's home an argument began. After just a few words they started toward each other and grappled violently, and the white man made desperate tries to put his finger in Bill Coe's eyes.

At that time old Bill ducked and caught the man's finger in his mouth, caught him around the throat and hit him three times in the side; and soon he found him limp in his arms. Bill was greatly excited, he feared something serious had happened; he eased the man to the ground. He soon revived, and when he was able to speak, he said, "I'm thru; I will never try to fight Bill Coe again."

Old Bill used to laugh and tell of an experience of log-splitting with his brother-in-law, Thomas Wilburn. They had a joint contract to finish a large number of rails. They cut down the trees, cut the logs and hauled them out to a handy place for work. Bill said, "Well Tom, if you can make as many rails as I can we will finish this job Monday." Tom's reply was, "I can make as many rails as you or any other damned man can!" "Let's go," was Bill's challenge.

Bill started off, working rapidly, and forgot about Tom. When he did come to himself and looked around to see what his helper was doing, he discovered that Tom was standing there looking at him work. When asked for an explanation Tom said, "Why Bill, I thought I could make rails, but since I see you at it, I concluded that you are in a class by yourself, and I got no business in the woods with you."

Calvin Coe told how his brother Bill carried a wagon around on his shoulders. Several young men had failed to lift it when Old Bill said as usual, "Move away, boys," then catching hold of the coupling-pole, put the whole thing on his shoulder and danced around, singing a song.

In all of these incidents related, Bill Coe had been very fortunate, but he had a serious accident. While driving a team, hauling logs, his hand was caught in a pulley and two fingers broken off.

Bill Coe was a peaceable man; his motto was, "Treat everybody right;" he believed in the truth and would not tell a lie even to avoid trouble; but he was brave and fearless. Tho only about five feet in height and weighing only one hundred forty-four pounds; he was a man of wonderful strength.

But because Bill was a physical giant and did not know the limit of his strength, he did not realize that there is a limit to human endurance, so Bill exhausted his great strength and finally became an invalid, at 45, and, during the last thirteen years of his life his wife and children had to care for him as for a child, helping him up and down, all of the time. He died at the age of fifty-eight, and his death was a severe loss not only to his family, but to the people of the community, for he had worked very hard to build up the interests of the Pea Ridge Colony. So, considering the life, the loyalty, the worth, the accomplishments of this man's life, one is inclined to adopt the language often used, and say, "Peace to his ashes."

CHAPTER FIVE
BEGINNING OF RACIAL STRIFE

In the year 1888, three white men, Charles Short, Ike Short and John Nealy began the strife that ended in the first blood-shed in the Pea Ridge Colony, and the Pea Ridge District, in spite of the fact that the majority of the citizens desired to live in peace and harmony. Perhaps these young men were not so much responsible, from a moral point of view, but the sad results were just the same, engendering ill-feeling among the people, and especially between the white and the Croutau.

These boys had not been properly trained; they knew nothing of honesty and justice; they grew up sitting around an old-fashioned fire-place, listening to others talk, especially planning how to stop the progress of the "Coe Tribe;" and they were influenced by such surroundings. Being shiftless and idle they had ample time to meditate on these things and to study mischief.

The boys of the "Coe tribe" never did seek trouble with anyone. They were peaceable, but they asked to be recognized as men and to be permitted to live and make their support, as others were doing. But, while they were for peace, and wanted to live in peace with all men, they were determined to defend their own rights, and in any way it might become necessary; and it was well understood that they would not bow and cringe before any man, since they were men, also.

Charles Short was a young man who had not used the privilege of going to school; he neglected his studies and often played truant; there were no truant officers in those days, so there was no influence to force him to remain in school; so he grew up to ignorance. Being thus lacking in intelligence and home training, he had very poor ideas of right and wrong, Ike Short grew up about as did Charley, but manifested better qualities and seemed considerably more civilized than his brother. Both being ignorant were dangerous as is true of all who are ignorant.

John Nealy was to be pitied, for his ignorance and his hereditary weakness, and even today, the writer of this story who is a descendant of those who were injured, has a feeling of pity for this poor fellow who never had a chance to be anybody. Born in a poor home, of a careless mother, and reared under worse conditions, it was but natural that he should go astray. Then, he was brought up without the care and guidance of a father, and influenced by evil associates who delighted in doing things that were wrong. He went from one farm to another, doing such work as he could secure; he was often idle, and of course had time to get into all kinds of mischief, and he did.

The young men, the Shorts, Taylors, Capps and others would drive recklessly around the District, especially thru the Coe settlement, cursing and using vile language. Sometimes they would tear down fences and do other things to annoy and to make trouble with the people of the settlement. The conduct of these young men in the Coe family was such as to arouse the men of the Colony to action, in defense of their rights, and the peace of their families, and that spirit was responsible for the resentment which precipitated the trouble with which this chapter deals, and the sad results of the interference of these mischief-makers.

Calvin Coe was a young man of about twenty-five years; a small man, weighing about one hundred thirty-five pounds; in color, he was yellow, or light brown, between the copper of the Indian and the yellow of the Chinese; his dark brown hair hung over his flat forehead; his set jaws gave evidence of a determination and a will unconquerable; and he was known to be a peaceable man, it was also known that he would not allow himself to be trampled without resentment and defense.

It was the custom of Calvin Coe to lie down and take a nap in the afternoon. And while he was trying to sleep, on this particular occasion, he heard one of the terrors passing crying:

"Buffalo Bill, from Bunker Hill.
Never was curbed, and never will!"

Being disturbed and angered by the fact that he knew this was intended to awaken him and annoy him, he forgot his determination to have peace, and hoping he could restrain himself, he rose up seized a gun and running toward the men who disturbed him, cried, "Lookout; here comes old hell!" Realizing the danger, and being unarmed, these men hurriedly left the place.

It is reported that, on this occasion, one of the brothers rode a horse and the other two were walking, and that when they saw Calvin with his gun, they rushed away and that the ones on foot outran the one on horseback. But, running, they were planning revenge, as the subsequent events will show.

The younger fellow Nealy ran home to his mother and told her of the occurrence, and how they had to run to save their lives. Milt's mother, a Miss Tump, was a woman of low morals and associated in an immoral way with the very worst characters of the Community, therefore, she had many friends among the tough element. Hearing her son's story, she became furious and said, "I will have the red-heads burning that Ridge before Saturday night." The "redheads" were the terrible Taylor boys, who got their living in a way that nobody seemed to know; but it was well known that they did not earn it by labor.

It is not known what the Nealy woman told the Taylors, but it was not long before one of them made his appearance in the Coe settlement, and it was known that trouble was near. This fellow went first; to the home of Mary Wilburn, and as was his custom; asked for food, saying with contempt, "Mary, can I have something to eat?" She answered, "My delight, Mr. Taylor," and soon had something ready. He refused to get down from his horse, saying, "I'll eat right here, where I am." She served the food on a plate, giving him bacon, beans, and corn bread. He soon ate all she had given him and demanded more. She served him again, and he went on his way. She thought she had avoided trouble with him, but, in this she was sadly mistaken, for he was determined to avenge the offense against his friends.

Taylor had not been gone very long before she heard her brother calling. "Oleson!" Recognizing the distress in his voice she knew that war had started, and she said, "Run, Oleson, for they have come to kill your uncle Calvin; you go right away and I'll be there soon." She knew that the fight would be to the finish and was determined that all should do their part, and allow no one to struggle alone. "But, mother, if I go they kill me, too," was Oleson's plea, but his mother urged him to rush on, and so he did.

When Taylor left Mary Wilburn's home, he went directly to her mother's, Patsy Ann, just over the hill, and there he ordered dinner. She told him it was after dinner hour, but she would fix him something. Knowing his disposition and trying to avoid trouble she called Calvin and told him to go to her daughter's house and get some meal.

"Yes mam," he answered, and started right away. Calvin was walking very rapidly, when, as he turned a corner and started up a hill, he heard someone calling him. Looking around he saw Will Taylor riding close behind him, and he knew he did not mean any good.

"Say, do you know anybody that's got any cattle to sell?" asked Taylor. After a moment's pause, Calvin answered, "Yes, my brother-in-law has two head to sell." He saw Taylor take a bottle of whiskey from his pocket, which bottle he handed to Calvin to take a drink. He knew that it was the custom of the Taylors to ask a man to drink, and if he did drink out of their bottle, when it was returned it would be broken over the head of the one who had taken the drink. He knew too, that if he refused to drink that would be considered an offense. So he drank.

Calvin Coe was surprised when Taylor did not attempt to hit him with the bottle; but while he was drinking, he saw him quickly draw two pistols. Knowing he had had no trouble with this man he wondered why he was trying to hurt him. With much anger, Taylor remarked, "You are the cattle I'm looking for; what's all this you have been saying about me?" "I have said nothing about you but a gentleman," Calvin answered. This Spirit of peace and the denial of the accusation did not satisfy Taylor, who had determined to do injury; so, at this time he thrust one pistol in the face of Calvin, pulled back the hammer and pulled the trigger; but, by some luck the shell did not explode. "Get into the road," ordered Taylor, and as he was unarmed, Coe knew it was best to obey. As he walked, the man riding along beside him kept striking at him, and his hands and arms were sore from the blows which were aimed at his head by Taylor, who was striking him with the butt of his gun.

Reaching a certain place Taylor ordered him to get down in the fence corner, and this order he refused to obey, for he had discovered Charley Short near there and knew that if he sat in the corner he would be shot in the back. After his refusal, in an angry, sneering voice, Taylor cried out, "Call up your damned crew!" "I have no crew," calmly insisted Calvin. It was at this time he called for Oleson, and was heard by his sister Mary Wilburn.

Calvin's mother, Patsy Ann was uneasy. She was waiting for his return with the meal, but she was listening, too, for she had seen Taylor turn his horse and ride in the direction which her son had gone. So, when she heard him call for Oleson, in that distressing voice, she knew he was in danger, and starting to him, she arrived about the same time as Mary Wilburn, Oleson, Ezekiel, and Ezekiel Junior arrived. When his sister Mary saw Taylor point his gun at Calvin and heard him demand, "Turn your pockets," she rushed up to her brother and cried, "Turn your pockets to no man, Cal Coe; turn your pockets to no man!"

These people, gathered about Taylor, were trying to make peace with him, urging him to stop and reason, and talk matters over. Seeing the danger, Patsy Ann Coe, white-haired, seventy years old, and very feeble, in her excitement, rushed up to Taylor and attempted to disarm him, lest he hurt her son. She grabbed one hand with the gun in it, and Ezekiel grabbed the other one, but Taylor was too strong for them. Ezekiel held to the hand which he had seized and actually took the gun which was in it; but Taylor thrust Patsy Ann from him and held on to the gun, in that hand.

During this struggle, a white man, Pat Pruett, had been sitting near and trying to make peace, Ezekiel, thinking he could trust him, handed him the gun he had taken from Taylor. Seeing this, Taylor turned his gun on Pruett and demanded the return of the one he was holding, and being fearful for his own safety, gave it back to Taylor. Things quieted down; Taylor seemed to be over his hot spell; Calvin Coe, thinking the danger passed, decided to go home, and turning walked away, Taylor raised his gun to shoot him in the back. Seeing this Ezekiel stopped, picked up a stone, hit Taylor's head, and the force was such that he fell forward and the gun was fired, the bullet hitting the ground near to Calvin Coe heels.

The crack of the gun and the flying dust from the bullet that had struck so near him, and which was intended to take his life aroused Calvin to the point that he rushed back, grabbed Taylor in the collar, and seized a stone with which he intended to bash his skull. It was at this moment that Charley Short ran from behind the fence, and began to fire, with two guns he held in his hands. Two shots took hold, Oleson Wilburn fell, with a bullet in his head and one in his arm. One bullet passed thru Patsy Coe's hair and another thru Ezekiel Junior's sleeve.

Mary Wilburn, tho a woman of forty-five or fifty, about five feet high, and about 145 pounds in weight, was very active, and she was willing to give her own life in protection of her family. Mary rushed forward and began hurling stones at Short, hitting him about the body with such force that he took to retreat. She called him a rogue, a sneak, a coward because he had sneaked from his hiding place and might have killed all of them but for the fact that his marksmanship was bad.

Calvin Coe, who had Taylor's back pinned to the ground, heard the crack of Short's gun and saw Oleson, his nephew fall. In his excitement, he left Taylor and, with his knife open began pursuing Charley Short who had begun running for his own life. Hearing screams he turned back and saw Taylor resting on his knees with his gun leveled at him. "I came here to kill you, Calvin Coe," came from Taylor. By some means, Taylor hesitated, as Calvin, looking him right in the eye moved nearer to him. Realizing that it was Taylor's life or his own, Coe leaped upon Taylor as a wild cat would leap, and they fought with terrible fury.

In less time than it requires to relate it, Calvin Coe grabbed Taylor, pulled his head back, and with his knife cut his throat from ear to ear. Then, turning from Taylor, lying on the ground and the blood gushing out of his wound, Coe started after Charley Short. Looking back, to his surprise, he saw Taylor, still on the ground, trying to fire his gun. He ran back quickly, seized the wounded man's gun and beat him over the head; and Taylor, the bully, the meddler, the intruder and the would-be murderer, went to sleep, never to wake again. In this incident, the Coe Colony witnessed the first fatal clash between the two races, there. Fortunately it resulted in only one death, for Oleson Coe's wound was not fatal.

To the members of the Colony, this was a matter of serious regret; they desired peace; they tried to live in peace; they tried to treat their neighbors right; and, above all, they did not want any one's life taken; but, all understood that it was a matter of one life or the other life, and they were glad that it was the life of Taylor, who had started the trouble rather than the life of Calvin Coe, the intended victim. But for all this love of peace, if they could have overtaken Charley Short they would have made an end to him, very quickly, they would have sent him on into eternity, with George Taylor.

Pat Pruett, who had witnessed the sad events, became excited and greatly afraid. He began crying, and said, "Aunt Pat, will they kill me, too?" Her reply was, "Why, Mr. Pruett, you have not harmed anybody; you tried to make peace, and no one will do you any harm. You may go in peace, but, as you go, and tell of this sad affair, be sure to tell the whole truth. Tell it that we did not want any trouble; that we desired peace; that we did not start the trouble; and that Mr. Taylor was killed while he was trying to kill my son. Tell the truth, Mr. Pruett, and as you have tried to make peace, today, and help us to keep peace in this District." He then mounted his horse and sped away like a cannonball.

In the southern part of the Colony there were many boys of ages ranging from twelve to fifteen years, and who had heard the firing of the guns, in the middle between the Coes the Taylor gang. They wanted to go to the rescue of their kinsmen. So, Jesse, Robert, Thomas E., and Joseph Coe, armed with a shot gun and a pistol, started to the scene of the trouble. They had not gone very far before they heard the sound of horse's feet and saw a man on a horse rapidly approaching.

One said, "They have killed all of grandmother's people, and they are getting away, so let's stop them." They jumped over the fence and hid in an orchard.

It was Pat Pruett, riding to tell the news, but they did not know the circumstances. They thought he was one of the killers, and were determined that he would not escape. Jesse Coe fired on Pruett as he rushed by, missed the man and shot his horse. The load hit the horse in the hip, and exciting him he increased his speed and was soon out of danger. No doubt that one shot that Jesse Coe made, that had helped to save the Colony from being wiped off the map; for after the death of Taylor and the shot at him, Pruett spread news that put the fear of the Lord into the hearts of many who might have been inclined to trample them.

When the pursuers could not overtake Charley Short, they returned to where George Taylor lay dead. Patsy Ann, the kind sympathetic mother that she was, went to Taylor, closed his mouth, folded his arms, using a bandana handkerchief her son Calvin gave her, to bind Taylor's mouth and hold his lips together. These acts of kindness to the dead, showed that these people bore no enmity, and they regretted the death even of this enemy who had tried to destroy them.

CHAPTER SIX
"DARK AND BLOODY GROUND"

―――◆―✕―◆―――

The tragic events of this chapter, the preceding one, and the Chronicles of the Pea Ridge Colony, during the perilous years of the reconstruction period are all in harmony with the name of Kentucky, according to the generally accepted definition — "dark and bloody ground!" Even now, at this distance from those early, furious days, feuds and strife among the Kentucky mountaineers show that the old spirit of retaliation and vengeance has not fully died. In this particular section the very ground still is "dark and bloody."

Jesse Coe, the lad of fifteen frequently mentioned in the preceding chapters not only was prominent in the affairs of this chapter, but he was prominent and foremost in many of the tragedies affecting the Coe Tribe. Thomas E. Coe, another one of the group of boys, grew up and for many years was principal of the public school. The way those events occurred may read very much like fiction, and some may be inclined to doubt them, but they are true, they are chronicles; not fiction, no matter how strange. Perhaps this is one of the instances in which it is true that "truth is stranger than fiction."

These boys left the orchard where they had fired on Pruett and went to where Taylor was killed and helped to convey the boy Oleson to his home, after which Jesse ran to Black's Ferry to tell his father what had happened, while Thomas, brother of the writer of these Chronicles carried to their home his story of the happenings.

At our home were three of us, Ada, Ora, and Samuel, the writer. I shall never forget how Thomas came in, all upset and said with great force, "Well, we laid one of them in the shade!" We did not ask any questions for we understood what he meant, but we were curious to go and see for ourselves. Having permission to go, we three children left the house together, and tho only eight years old at that time, I remember very vividly the things which we saw and heard.

On our way we stopped at the home of Aunt Patsy Coe, who had a daughter about fifteen, named Mollie. She stooped over and said to us in an mean tone, "Your Uncle Calvin has killed a man and now will go to hell." Arriving at the home of Patsy Coe we found Oleson lying there, his arm extended and the blood dripping freely from his wound. Our uncle Calvin Coe was walking back and forth using bad words of language. We heard him say to Oleson," If you had been turning and fighting instead of standing like a statue, you would not have been shot." But the wounded boy's only answer was a cry of agony.

We made our way to where the dead man was. Taylor was lying on the ground, head pointing north and feet pointing south, and grandmother was sitting and using the branch of a peach tree to keep the flies from his face, showing mercy to, and sympathy for, the man who had been so cruel as to seek the death of her own children; and one could imagine that to her own tender, sympathetic heart, she was praying the dying prayer of the Divine Nazarene, "Father forgive them, for they know not what they do!"

Bill Coe chided his brother Calvin for what had happened, saying, "Well, you got yourself in trouble at last," to which Calvin replied, "Yes, Bill; I had to kill him;" and all who are familiar with the story narrated know that it was true, that it was a life for a life.

The writer was a boy of eight years and was not allowed to listen to the councils held, but he remembered how they gathered into little groups and discussed what was best to do under the circumstances. Finally it was decided that Cal Coe should surrender himself, go to jail and await trial by the court since he had killed Will Taylor in self-defense. Calvin went on to jail accompanied by a number of the men, while others took Oleson to Mud Camp, where his brothers were, in order that he might have protection also. No effort was made to harm either Calvin or Oleson, and it is well, for those who were with them were prepared to defend them to the bitter end.

Now, it was Pat Pruett who quickly carried to the Taylor boys news of the killing of their brother and on hearing it they raved and wailed like women. One suggested, "Let's go and kill the whole damned pack." Another argued, "They will be expecting us and will be prepared, so let's wait till they forget, then we can wipe out the whole lot without danger to ourselves." Then, they remembered that they must first secure their brother's body and give it a burial.

When the Taylors requested a friend who was an undertaker, to accompany them and assist in securing the body of their brother, he said, "You boys had better stay here and allow me to go, cause they ain't got nothin' agin me, and they might kill you." This was agreed on and he went on the sad mission. They avoided the present danger, but down in their hearts these men were determined to avenge the death of their brother, tho he had lost his life in an effort to take other lives, the lives of men who had done them no ill. They were determined to destroy those who wanted peace with the neighbors; who were willing to make any reasonable sacrifice for peace; whose chief ambition was to improve their own condition and prove themselves worthy of confidence and respect of their neighbors of all classes. These people sincerely regretted the sad occurrence, and none more than Calvin Coe, who had been compelled to take a life in order to save his own life.

Saturday, Sunday and Monday passed quietly; in the colony there was no disturbance; but all know the danger and understood that the quiet was but the calm before the storm. Knowing this they are prepared for what might come. They regretted mortal strife and would have welcomed any other kind of adjustment of differences. In their hearts was no hatred even toward their enemies who was conspiring to destroy them; but they understood they had the right of every individual to defend himself and his own; and for this they were fully prepared; they were prepared for the inevitable!

A fair minded white man who knew of the plot to murder members of the Colony went secretly to Mary Wilburn's home and informed her that the Taylor boys and their gang would be there that very night; and they would bring oil, set the houses on fire and then would shoot the people as they ran out. Giving this information he said, "Mary, you and your people have been kind to me, moreover, you did not begin this trouble, and under the circumstances I consider it my duty to warn you that you all have a show for your lives." He added, "You live for peace, but you have a right to defend yourselves if they try to take your life." This said, he walked away.

Mary sent each one of her seven children in a different direction to warn the members of the Colony of the danger. They came together, took counting and loaded their guns, arranged their plans, assigned duties to the different men of the tribe, and, tho many loved peace, they were prepared for war with those who sought to kill them. This group of defenders consisted of two men, and four boys ranging in age from 14 to 17 years. They hid themselves in a corn field nearby and waited with determination to defend themselves and their own or to give up their lives in the attempt to do so. With this determination they awaited the coming of the mob. Perhaps they prayed;

perhaps they did not; but it is certain that they felt no condemnation of conscience because they were doing what every individual has a right to do.

It was scarcely dark when Mandy Coe, mother of the writer, looking thru an opening between the logs of the house imagined she saw the mob cautiously approaching. As she told it she could almost hear their "tramp, tramp" as they moved nearer and nearer to her home with intention to destroy it. Fearing consequences she took the small children, quickly went out the back door, ran to the woods nearby, and there awaited the results, knowing that the brave defenders would do their part, yet fearing that some of them would be killed, also.

Anxiously the men awaited the coming of the mob. It was Thomas Coe who said, "Often as the clouds passed between us and the moon, we imagined we saw many men, when there were only shadows. At last the assassins came, moving quietly down the lane toward the house, walking two abreast, each with his gun tightly clutched. The defenders had placed themselves near the fence, and suddenly Bill Raspberry, that grand old man, arose, gun in hand and asking no questions, his "trigger finger" began to move. Following his example the other guns began to flash death, and the members of the mob, forgetting that they had guns began a rapid and a disorderly retreat, amid great confusion.

In giving their version of the affair, some of the members said they thought some of their number had turned traitor and were firing on their comrades; others declared the shots came so fast that they did not have time to find out from what direction they came. One thing was certain, someone had given warning and the men were prepared to defend themselves and their homes. No houses were burned, and no one was killed, but the members of the mob were with heaviness in their hearts, because they had attempted to take life — the lives of innocent people who want them no harm and who desired to live in peace with them.

Not long after the mob had been halted, pretending to be on a friendly mission, fourteen white men, known to be members of the night-raiders, returned to the home they had intended to burn and spoke to Luzette. When she refused to go to them they convinced her they were for peace and that they wouldn't hurt a hair on her head. The spokesman explained to her that a white woman wanted her to do some work for her, and they had come to bring the woman. But, uneducated as they were, and as peace-loving as they had been, it was impossible to convince anyone that it required fourteen men, with guns in their hands, to carry a simple message concerning work.

The majority of the young people were gathered at Patsy Ann's home, and among them, Thomas Wilburn and John Coe, both of whom were with those who disappointed and routed the mob. When Billy Wilburn put in his appearance, old man Thomas then laughed for joy, at seeing his son alive. Thomas said to Billy, "Now, Billy, you go home and I'll come along soon." And Billy told the others goodbye and started home, with no worry there would any harm come to him or that anyone would try to harm him.

As Billy tells it, he was trotting along thru the woods when he heard the report of a gun and saw the tree near him splintered by a bullet. Frightened, he began to run, and as he ran bullets flew around him and plowed the ground near his feet as he sped forward. Billy then was certain that some of the gang was after him and they had decided to take his life. He was sure it was George Taylor whose brother had been killed, who was trying to kill him as a part of revenge against the Colony.

Billy related that as he sped away as fast as he was able to do, someone called him by name and in imitation of his father's voice. He knew there was an effort to deceive him and stop him, in order to have opportunity to kill him; so, disregarding the voice, he rushed on trying to get away from the danger. Thus Billy made his way to Mud Camp to warn those there of the efforts of the enemies.

On his way to Mud Camp, Billy met his grandfather, and accosted him with "Hello, grandpa." The old man returned the greeting saying jovially, "Why, hello, Billy." Then, seeing that his grandson was terribly excited he asked, "Well, what has happened?" Breathing and talking rapidly Billy recited, "The mob was on the hill last night but we managed to stop them and keep them from burning our houses or killing anybody, but they done come back round, now, and want to kill everybody, and I was runnin' on to tell you."

With his usual fervor, the old man cried, "Blame my liver, boy, come on and we will defend our homes or die a tryin'." So the old man led the way back, running so rapidly that Billy could hardly keep up with him. Another council was held and everyone was pledged to fight in defense of their lives and their homes, and for the helpless women and innocent children of the Colony.

John Coe, a boy of seventeen and one of those who arrested the mob near the home of Mary Wilburn, thought it best to get away from the scene of conflict, so, securing some of his grandmother's clothes, he left the house in female attire, but, soon slipped off his disguise and went running toward Mud Camp to bear the news of what had happened. On his way he met old man Zeek and Billy on their way to the Colony. John argued with the old man that it would not be wise to go on because the men were well armed and would surely kill him, but the old hero roared, "If I die it's all right, but I'm going to fight for my people; and I'm going right now!" But this boy John argued with the old man and convinced him it would be better to wait and let the law take its course, never thinking that this same lawless mob would one day take his own life without thought of law, of courts, of judges, nor of notice. So old man Zeek returned to Mud Camp still hoping and praying for peace among the people, for all the people; for in spite of his willingness to defend his own, in his heart he hated no one, envied no one and certainly did not want to injure anyone.

CHAPTER SEVEN
WHEN JUSTICE WAS NOT BLIND

"For right is right, since God is God,
And right the day shall win;
To doubt would be disloyalty,
To falter would be sin."

The trial of Calvin Coe, for the killing of Will Taylor was brief and without the serious consequences feared. No mob was formed; there was no effort at intimidation; no threats were heard; and there was no hostile demonstration against the Coes and their friends; and there was a sense of relief when it was over.

To begin with, there was no witnesses for the prosecution, because, the only witnesses were those implicated, and their testimony would have condemned themselves and helped the defense, therefore, the prosecuting attorney confessed that he had no witness to present. All the witnesses for the defense agreed in their testimony which was to the effect that Taylor started the trouble; that Calvin Coe and the others did try to avoid any serious consequences; and finally that Cal Coe killed Will Taylor when there was no other way to save his own life.

"Calvin Coe," called the constable, and Cal Coe stood before the judge, raised his hand and took the usual oath to "tell the truth and nothing but the truth, so help me God." "Calvin Coe," began the judge, "you are charged with killing a man, namely, William Taylor, for which crime you are to answer. Killing a man is murder; the penalty for murder is death; now, how do you plead, guilty or not guilty?"

With little hesitation and unusual deliberation Coe answered, "Your honor, judge, I am not guilty of murder, for two reasons. First, I had nothing against the man I confess that I killed, and I have heard it said that murder is killing, "with malice aforethought," and I understand that to mean with something against the man killed. Then, judge, I killed Mr. Taylor when he was trying to kill others, and only then when he would have killed me, and my life was as dear to me as his life to him. In all ages and according to all laws of God and of men, it is not a crime to take a life to save your own life. For these reasons, Judge Stone, I confess I killed Will Taylor, yet declare I am innocent of the crime of murder and ought not to be punished."

When Calvin Coe was dismissed from the witness box a white man came rushing forward and cried, "Judge, your honor, I have a message for you; it is from the Taylor boys." As the judge did not interrupt him he continued, "The Taylor boys sent me to tell you that they do not ask any judge or any court to settle their affairs, that they will settle them all with their guns; and I tell you they are prepared to do it, too."

Judge Stone had heard the testimony of Patsy Ann, Calvin's mother. Mary Wilburn, whose house the mob tried to burn, old man Ezekiel and Zeek Junior, all telling how Taylor had begun the trouble that ended in his death, and how Calvin Coe had killed only to save his own life. By these the judge was deeply impressed. He was especially impressed with the fact that the prosecution had not one word of testimony to contradict these witnesses for the defense. Then he gave due weight to the message from the Taylors, which message he believed to be authentic and which was evidence of the lawless spirit of those who sent it. And, when the prosecution had no evidence to present in rebuttal, the judge reached a conclusion and rendered his decision.

"Well," began the judge, "it is a terrible thing to kill a man, to take what you can never restore; killing with premeditation and with malice aforethought is murder in the first degree and this crime is punishable by death." "But," continued Judge Stone, "a man has the right to protect his home and to defend himself against violence attempted against him; and, in doing this he has the right to kill, if necessity requires it, for his home is his castle and his life is as dear as is that of the one who attempts to kill him."

At this point in the proceedings there was great excitement and great anxiety. It had been generally conceded that Will Taylor was the aggressor; that he forfeited his life when he tried to kill another; that he "got what was comin' to him," but it had been freely boasted that no white judge would dare to set free a man of the subordinate race who had under any circumstances killed a white man. Moreover, after the testimony of the white man that the Taylors would "settle their own trouble with their guns," it was feared that they might begin right away, if Calvin Coe should be acquitted. But, in spite of all this, from the remarks of the judge, the people anticipated him and expected a verdict of acquittal; and they feared the consequence.

The Coe relatives and sympathizers were uneasy. They had noted the rise of prejudice; had witnessed the change in the attitudes of the whites in general, from that of friendliness to one of extreme hostility; they were aware that the Taylor gang had friends and sympathizers who approved and encouraged their depredations against the

"Croutaus" and, for these reasons much of their faith in the honor, honesty and fairness of white people had been lost. Thus, they all sat fearing and trembling, while the trial was in process, and especially as the judge was summing up the facts in the case.

It was well known and fully admitted by the prosecution that there were no witnesses against Calvin Coe; that in this case, not one of those who had sought his life and the lives of others dared to come out in the open and defend their actions. They were satisfied that elementary justice, common fairness, honest opinion, the constitution of the United States and of the State of Kentucky all would justify what had been done; yet, because of their inferior position as a group, they were "fearful and unbelieving." This was the status of affairs as Judge Stone continued his summary.

"Stand up, Calvin Coe," ordered the Judge, and then he continued: "It appears from the evidence in this case that in killing William Taylor you were within your rights; that you were protecting others whom he was trying to harm; and it seems conclusive, also, that you were defending your own life which would have been taken had you not killed Taylor first. It is generally accepted and is consonant with justice that every individual has the right to kill another in defense of his own life, and not one witness has appeared to contradict your testimony or refute your contention that you did kill in defense of your own life; and this the prosecution admits to be true, in the case."

There had been absolute quiet from the beginning of the statement by Judge Stone, and yet, plainly could be seen the difference of attitude on the part of those making up the crowd in the court room. Those who were in sympathy with the defendant or in favor of equal justice smiled approval and gave evidence of relief as they followed the trend of expressions by the court. On the other hand, on the countenance of others could be plainly seen evidence of displeasure and disapproval, and their desire that the defendant should be condemned and punished despite the preponderance of evidence to prove him justifiable in what had been done.

After a brief pause, during which time he took a sip of water, from a glass near him, Judge Stone continued, saying, "This defendant belongs to a race or a group of people who, for more than two hundred years served the other and dominant group as abject slaves. You will note that I say group, using this as a substitute for race, because, in the veins of these people will be found the blood of all races under the sun; and, with some measure of humiliation and shame I might add that they are not responsible for this diversity of racial lineage, since it was forced upon them by those who in everything whatever, dominated their wills, their actions, and their very lives."

The wavering of Judge Stone's voice gave evidence of the intensity of his feelings, as he insisted, "Because of what I have just cited, we of the dominant race or group, we who held the others in bondage; we who through the long period of their bondage heaped indignities upon them; we who even yet fear them, persecute them and obstruct their progress should not forget that actually we are trampling our own flesh and blood! And we should remember that even savages are not accustomed to destroy their own."

Then came from the judge the most startling utterances to which those people had ever listened. Raising his hand with index finger pointed and his hand trembling, he urged with great vehemence, "These people are human beings and are entitled to all the rights, privileges, opportunities and immunities provided by law and conceded to others of our citizenry. The man with white skin is no more a citizen than is he of the darker hue; and the latter is entitled to the same consideration as the former. This is law; it is equity; it is common, even-handed, unprejudiced justice; and, as far as I am concerned, as long as I can, by word or deed influence human opinion and human action, and as long as it is my privilege to judge between man and man, I shall do my best to see that justice is meted out to all alike."

Doing the unusual thing of rising from his seat to render a

decision, Judge Stone said, "Calvin Coe, since the evidence in this case convinces me that in killing William Taylor you were within your natural and constitutional rights; that you were defending your own life which was as dear to you as the other man's life was to him, the conclusion of the court is that you were justifiable in all that you have done; therefore, it is the decision of the court that you be acquitted of the charge of murder and immediately discharged from custody."

In the presence of all and in a voice loud and strong so that all could hear him, Judge Stone concluded, "And, since the information comes that the brothers of the man you killed will not recognize the verdict of the court but intend to take vengeance in their own way, the court grants to you the right to arm yourself for defense, and, if you must, kill others who may seek your life."

Living at this time, under these more favorable conditions and especially in the more law-abiding sections of our country it is difficult to understand the events herein recorded. Many doubtless are surprised at the attitude and the actions of Judge Stone. Perhaps some could be inclined to doubt that such a man could be found, under those trying and dangerous circumstances would take such a position and declare so strongly for human rights — but there have been sceptics in all ages and this one surely is not an exception to the rule of human conduct.

Today there are those of the dominant group who have no sympathy for the submerged element in our body politic. They consider that there is no consideration due those who are the progeny of the slaves whom their ancestors lashed and trampled. Many of them are ruthless, unfeeling and cruelly unjust! On the other hand, there are thousands of the other group who have no faith in the justice or fairness of the dominant element. Their contention is that all are haters of the darker peoples; that they are hypocritical in all their expressions and actions; and they meet every effort at friendliness with rebuffs and undisguised hostility.

However, as Judge Stone was a representative of many of his

group who insisted that justice be accorded to all, so we have, even in the most prejudiced section of America, men and women who are justice-loving, peace-making, and who, in the matter of racial oppression "have never bowed their knees to Baal nor kissed his grotesque image." These individuals do not measure a man by the color of his skin nor the texture of his hair, nor yet by the circumstances of his birth. They are God's true noblemen; the salt that will save this nation from the festering influence of racial hatred, strife and oppression.

In fairness it must be admitted also, that among the descendants of the slaves there are lovers of peace and of their fellow-men, who match in kind the faith, friendship and justice of the dominant group. And the hope for the ultimate peace and permanent prosperity lies in the mutual respect, confidence and cooperation of these right-thinking, justice-loving members of both the dominant and the submerged group among us — they must be the "little leaven that shall make leaven the whole of our aggregate citizenship constituency." But now we will return to the story and go on with the "Chronicles of the Coe Colony."

CHAPTER EIGHT
A TRAIN OF EVENTS
"Coming Events Cast Their Shadows"

———◆◆◆———

At Patsy Ann's house, the morning after the mob had been there, John, who had helped to halt the mob, remained in seclusion, with gun in hand, ready to meet the enemies if they should come again. At Luzette's house, where the fourteen men had laid their guns on the fence and declared their peaceable intentions there was much unrest as well as great anxiety, especially because Bill Raspberry, the grand old man had been wounded, was suffering greatly, and they feared further trouble. This wounded hero crawled to an opening in the wall, with gun in hand, and there he watched diligently for the approach of the enemy, determined still to do his part. From his hiding place he had watched the enemies and only relaxed when he saw them depart.

Things were peaceable at Bill Coe's house, therefore, Mandy who had sent out the warning the night before, was standing in the northwest corner of the garden, looking toward other houses of the Colony and wondering if any of her kinsmen had been killed the night before, by the cruel, heartless mob. Standing there she saw her son Thomas, a boy of thirteen coming toward her, and, running to him she asked anxiously if any of their kinfolk got killed. Thomas informed her that all escaped except Raspberry and that he was not seriously hurt. He told how the old man had been watching until the gang had gone, and expressed the hope and belief that they would not return to molest anybody.

When his mother spoke of her regrets that they must do as they were, and must go prepared to kill people, against the laws of God, this boy of tender years expressed himself in language surprisingly mature for one of his age. He said, "Mother, we want peace and will do all we can to have it, but the fathers and mothers of the white children have told them that we have no right to live. They have taught them to hate us and to fear us as they would a snake, and to kill us too, as they would a snake; so we must kill, if we would save our own lives."

In these words this mere boy expressed the sentiments of the members of the Coe Tribe and their determination. He gave voice to the cause that underlies all the race hatred and race strife, when he expressed himself concerning the wickedness of parents who teach their children to hate other children who are different from them. This is a brigther day. Much of the animosity of other days has passed. Those who were slave-holders and those who were slaves have passed into eternity, with few exceptions; but there still are people who teach their children to hate. And it is certain that the seeds of hatred thus sown in the minds of children will most certainly bear fruit in future strife, perhaps in a war of races which will tremendously retard human progress.

Now, after Calvin Coe had been acquitted and given permission to arm for his protection, he left the courtroom relieved, yet uneasy, for he knew his life would be constantly in danger; that efforts would be made to kill him, at any time. So this man, marked for slaughter, immediately placed an order for two Winchester rifles, one for himself and one for his brother, Ezekiel Junior.

Although this brother Ezekiel walked with a crutch as result of injury sustained in the army during the Civil War, he was supposed to have stabbed Will Taylor in the back during the fight which ended fatally for Taylor, so Ezekiel was also marked for slaughter and must need be always on guard. After receiving their arms both brothers considered themselves in position to defend their lives and were determined to do so, well aware that if they were caught off guard no mercy would be shown and any quarter given.

Most intimate was the friendship and the association between Calvin Coe and John Coe, known as "Little John," to distinguish between him and the elder John Coe, called "Old John." Perhaps the true story of the friendship and loyalty of these two friends will never be written, but they, like David and Jonathan were friends in life or in death. Like Damon and Pythias, they loved each other, trusted each other, and would not have hesitated to die, the one for the other.

John, the son of Bill Coe, was born in 1870. At the time of this story, John was about eighteen years of age, a strong fellow, and tho only 5 feet, seven inches in height and weighing only one hundred fifty pounds, he was one of the strongest men of the community; and he had a strong will, as well as a strong body. After Cal Coe purchased his rifle, John bought one also, and they were almost invariably seen together, each with his gun in his hand or under his arm. It was said that they had entered into an "offensive and defensive alliance," and the developments justify the conclusion.

Because these two comrades were generally together and were always armed, they were not molested, for all knew what would be the consequences, that someone would die. During the whole year after the killing of Will Taylor they had no trouble and the Coe Colony had peace, both at headquarters and at Mud Camp.

As is true of all human experiences, and as had been often true among the Coe Tribe, romance entered into their life again, the events occurring into connection with life at Mud Camp, often mentioned, a little community about fourteen miles northwest of the main Colony. This was an important part of the main Colony, because two sons of Ezekiel Coe, loved, courted and married two girls, sisters, and settled there. Joe, having gone to Mud Camp seeking work and to better opportunities met a girl named Tildy, and her sister whose name was Tennessee. Joe fell in love with Tildy and they were married, after a very brief courtship. When Joe returned home he told his brother about Tennessee, Tildy's sister, and not long after that John and Tennessee were joined in wedlock.

From these two brothers and their loyal wives came a number of children to swell the number of the Colony, to fight their battles, and to suffer, as is brought out in this story of the ups and downs, good and evil fortunes, successes and failures, joys and sorrows, and the prosperity and adversity of these most remarkable people whose history will compare in richness, devotion to high ideals, courage and loyalty, with the best of human breeds. Joe's children were Oscar, the first born, Burtie, second, and Della, who was but a little tot when her father was maliciously killed, his death being one of the list of tragedies here related and described.

The children of John Coe and Tennessee were Cory, who died at the age of ten; Isabel, who was burned to death while playing near the fire; and the third was a boy whom they called Chester, and who was a baby when his mother died from grief over the child whose end was so tragic and so untimely. After John Coe lost his wife, his home became "bachelor's quarters," with Cal Coe and the two Johns as occupants; and these two young men were single and waiting to be captured by some fair maidens. They were not foolish enough to demand perfection in the girls they were to make their wives, but they wanted to find girls who would be loyal and true and make their hearts and their homes happy.

Again Cupid got in his shot and Calvin became the lover of Mollie Ballard, while John Coe's heart was captured by a girl named Nan Anderson. Nan was a white woman and according to the laws of Kentucky could not be married to John, because he was classed as "colored" so, it was decided that they would go to Indiana to be married and that Calvin and Mollie would join them and make it a double wedding. Then, "Old John" decided that he would go along and see the job well done.

For the purpose mentioned, the five; two brides, two grooms and "Old John" walked twenty-five miles over dusty roads to Glasgow, Kentucky where they were to board the train for Indiana. They reached Glasgow just as the day was dawning, and Mollie, looking back cried, "Look children the morning star is rising on us." Soon they saw the people rushing on to their daily toil, and they were happy in the thought that soon they would be where the law of the land would not deal unjustly with them by making a difference between races.

Those young people always charged to "Old John" the disappointment that came to them just when they were about to take the step that would have brought them so much of happiness and joy, for it was following his advice that caused the trouble. It was this way: As they had considerable time before the arrival of the train, the old man suggested that they go to the home of a woman whom he knew and have breakfast before beginning their journey. To this all consented and accordingly followed him to this home. In eating the girls pulled off their gloves and their dark veils revealing their identity, and that was the cause of the trouble.

They were all on the train and it was time for the train to start, when a white man, George Reed rushed in and grabbed one of the boys demanding, "Where are you going?" Receiving the reply, "It is no business of yours where we are going," he became abusive and the other boy pulled out his knife with which to defend against the attack.

Old John came running in with his gun drawn on the intruder, when Reed opened his coat and revealed the badge of an Officer of the law, and placed all three of them under arrest, ending their wedding trip and disappointing them greatly.

These men were within their rights; they had broken no law and done nobody harm; there was no law to prevent them from passing from one state to another; they were arrested and abused for no cause whatever. They could have resisted and could have overpowered and killed Reed, but such was the respect they had for the law and such their desire to have peace, that they submitted to this injustice rather than cause trouble and possible blood-shed. They went back to Mud Camp, and suffered other indignities and humiliations in the interest of peace — for their own sake and the sake of others who might have suffered if they had resisted the efforts to degrade them. In spite of this docile, peaceful spirit, these people who were inoffensive, often felt the iron heel of those whose blood flowed thru their veins.

Even today, the descendants of these peaceable "Croutaus" and others of the fraternity of oppression, these who are the direct descendants of the slaves who helped to make America, constitute the submerged element of our American Social System. Today, also it is true that they are least considered and more abused and persecuted than any other class of citizenry; and still they remain, for the most part, loyal to the country, peaceable and law abiding, despite the contention otherwise.

At the trial Calvin and John were set at liberty, because there was no charge against them, but "Old John" was made to pay a fine of fifty dollars for pulling his gun on an officer. They all came out of jail in good spirits, Calvin and John picking a banjo and singing a new song they had composed during their days in jail. The song was entitled "Mollie and Nan, and Cal and John."

CHAPTER NINE
THE GRIM REAPER REAPS
"Death Loves a Shining Mark"

Again the members of the Coe Colony were called to bow their heads in sorrow, to go to the graveyard and hear the solemn words, "Earth to earth and dust to dust," and see one of their number covered over with earth, and leave him there

"Under the sod and the dew,
Waiting the judgment day."

This deep sorrow was caused by the murder of young Oleson Wilburn one of the bravest of the brave and one the Colony could scarcely afford to spare. It will be remembered that Oleson was wounded when Will Taylor was killed; on several occasions efforts had been made to kill him; but "they got him at last," as a member of the gang was reported to have said, and the "grim reaper" had thrust in his sickle and reaped again.

As the old man told the story, "Old Zeek" and Oleson started down to Mud Camp to care for the house and the property of "Old John," while he and the young folks were going on the wedding trip to Indiana. They started the very day the others left home. They traveled together until they came to where there was a "fork in the road," and stopped to decide which road would be nearer, as both led near to Mud Camp. Finally, it was decided that the old man would travel by the right-hand road and Oleson would take the one turning to the left. Here they parted, expecting to meet a little later at Mud Camp; but it was the last time the old man saw Oleson alive.

Only the books of the Recording Angel will ever reveal how, when, and where Oleson died, for if there were eye-witnesses they were never found, or their lips were sealed, sealed by fear of having the same fate overtake them. There were many reports and plausible theories but none that might be reasonably called authentic, since only an eye-witness could give full and accurate information. The following is the version which seems the most plausible.

Soon after Oleson had left his grandfather, he met or was overtaken by two men who required of him to halt and soon informed him that he must die, and his pleadings were all in vain. The report has it that the young man argued, "Why take my life when I have done you no harm? I am innocent of any crime and don't deserve to die. You had better stop and think and consider if I have done anything to have to die for. If you have grievance against any one else, then why make me suffer for that?" But to this they gave no heed, answering with curses and sneers.

According to the unauthenticated story one man snapped his gun five times with it pointed toward Oleson's heart, and swore when the gun failed to fire. He then pointed his other gun at the man who was with him and demanded that he shoot Oleson. This man contended that he came along to stand guard and not to kill anybody and that he did not intend to do so. But the murderer insisted and swore that if he did not shoot the boy he himself would be killed. It seemed that this man was in deadly fear of the other one, therefore he pointed his gun and fired, and Oleson fell.

Old Ezekiel made his way to Mud Camp and waited in vain for Oleson, but he never came. The news went back to the others of the Colony, but no trace of him could be found, though they feared the worst. No one of them knew whether he was dead or alive. Three weeks later his body was found in the dense forest, far from any highway. He had been buried in a shallow grave and in the clothing which he wore when he left his mother's home for Mud Camp. This sad news of the disappearance of Oleson greeted the travelers when they reached Mud Camp on the return from Glasgow.

The killing of Oleson Wilburn was unprovoked and absolutely inexcusable. He was kindly disposed; he loved and honored his parents; he was a good, jolly, friendly fellow; he was for peace, and not only tried to live in peace with others but he often tried to make peace where there was strife between neighbors. But of course, enmity, prejudice and jealousy take no account of excellent qualities; so peaceable Oleson was killed as an act of vengeance against the colony.

The thing which puzzled the Colony was the report that this boy had surrendered and suffered himself to be murdered without making effort to save his life or to kill in defense of his life. It was a part of the compact among the members of the Colony that under no circumstances would one of them submit to such without fighting; that they would fight with the last measure of strength and try to carry another to judgment. They concluded that this part of the story could not be true; but they renewed their determination to stick together and to protect one another to the bitter end.

The provocation and the justification of the attitude of these people and their grim determination to sell their lives as dearly as possible may be better understood by consideration of the incidents connected with and immediately following the death of Joe Coe, brother of Old John and brother of Calvin the brave fighter and defender of his kinfolks. They will also give information as to the cowardly methods of those who would kill without giving an individual any show for his life; who were mean enough to burn houses and destroy women and children.

This hero, Joe, had gone from Mud Camp to spend the night at his mother's home in the Pea Ridge Colony. He arose early in the morning, curried and fed his horses, put the harness on them and was ready to start on his return trip to Mud Camp, fourteen miles distant. He was peaceable, and in spite of all that had happened and all his people had been caused to suffer, he hated no one, bore no ill will, had never tried to injure anybody; and therefore he had no thought that there would be any attempt to kill him.

On his way from the barn back to the house to bid his mother goodbye he heard the sharp report of a gun. Unsuspecting, he stood trying to find out from what direction the sound came, and, in the early morning light he saw the figure of a man. There was another report and Joe was stunned by a bullet that struck him. He rushed on to the house while the bullets were whizzing around him and plowing the ground at his feet. Reaching the house, Joe got his brother's gun and tried to use it, but not understanding it he was unable to fire it at his murderer. Weakened by loss of blood and suffering great pain, he soon dropped down with the gun still in his hand.

As Joe fell, the old man, Ezekiel sprang from his bed and closed the door, and just as he did a bullet shattered the door and dropped on the floor at his feet. Perhaps there were a hundred bullets fired, falling all around, yet only one person was killed, all of which seemed like a miracle. Joe requested that they send for his family, but he died before the news of the assault reached them at Mud Camp.

When Joe cried, "Mother, I am going to die, send after my family," his mother said, hysterically, "Oh Joe, if you are going to die, you must pray; you must pray the Lord to forgive your sins and save your soul." Suffering excruciating pain Joe cried, "But I won't pray; let the one that took my life be responsible for my sins." "But that can't be," urged his mother; "for you must pray for yourself; for your own sins." Gasping and dying, murdered for no just cause, Joe made this final statement: "I can't pray, but I do hope that some of you will see to it that my children are carried away from among these savage people."

Joe Coe died; the grim reaper had reaped again; and thus ended the life of another brave but peaceful citizen who did no harm to any one and bore nobody ill, who, like others of the Pea Ridge Colony wished and sought peace and good will toward men. In the death of this, another innocent man, by the hands of ruthless assassins were sown seeds which, in after years brought a mighty harvest of strife, hatred, sorrow, and blood-shed as will be recorded in the further "Chronicles of the Coe Colony."

Soon it was known all over the Colony that another attempt had been made to wipe them out; that another of their number had been added to the list of those already slain; that the unknown murderers slipped away as quietly as they came and no one of their number suffered; and this report caused another dark shadow to settle over this community which already had suffered such deep, heart-rending sorrow.

Again the sentiment and the uncompromising attitude of the whole Colony are expressed by one of its representative members. This time it is Calvin Coe. When he was informed of his brother's death, he uttered this sad lament: "I wish I had been there to help my brother. They mighty have got me, but I am sure I would have got some of them, too. I have not hated anybody; I never desired to harm anyone; the man I killed was doing his best to kill me and I had to kill him to save my own life." He added, "They killed my nephew when he was without anything to defend himself with; now, they have killed my dear brother, and before God their time will come to pay! I will always be prepared to defend myself, and if they want to kill me, I hope they will come and fight it out with me and not just sneak around and kill my friends and kinfolks. I am prepared and I'll ask no favors and grant none, so help me God!"

One of the first things in the program of better preparation was to cut down the trees and the underbrush composing the thicket near the house where Joe was killed and the decision to remove every such place as might afford a hiding place for the enemies. There was the renewal of the compact that all would stand together in defense of their collective and individual rights and sell their lives as dearly as possible. Who could condemn this attitude? Who could say it was wrong? It was in keeping with that ancient, universally accepted dictum that "Self-preservation is the first law of nature;" and who can say that this is not justice, and equity?

Old man Ezekiel did not long survive his son, Joe. The excitement of the tragedy and the grief over the loss of Joe proved too much for the weary old soul, and he soon bade farewell to earth and its ties and passed into the realm of eternal peace, "Where the wicked cease to trouble and where the weary are at rest."

After the death of his father, John Coe, "Old John," decided to move back to Pea Ridge in order to care for his mother who was growing old and was breaking under the strain of the tragedies which had followed so closely one upon another. He also deemed it best that the men of the Colony should be nearer to each other in interest of mutual protection and defense. Shortly after his return to the Pea Ridge section of the Colony his wife bore a son to him great happiness. But this happiness was of short duration, for quite shortly after the birth of the child, the mother passed into eternity, leaving him heart-broken.

In addition to the children born in the homes of the Coe Colony there came others in a peculiar way. For instance, while "Old John" was living in his bachelor quarters there came to his home a woman by the name of Mary Evans bringing with her baby girl, shut up in a "valise," as they called them in that day. Nobody knew whence they came nor whose was the child. However, "Old John" would not allow them to be homeless, so he took and gave them shelter. This little girl whom they named "Larra" grew up in intimate association with the Colony and was married and brought into the world ten children who shared the fortunes and destinies of the Coe Tribe.

CHAPTER TEN
THE WAR BREAKS OUT ANEW

When the old man John moved his family back to the Coe Colony that brought back also the inseparable comrades, John and Calvin. As usual they were together, and as usual each had his Winchester rifle with him. For two years after their return, there was peace in the Colony, and tho there were frequent reports of what George Taylor said he would do, the people had come to believe that peace had come to them, at last. But the boys would not relax their vigilance and would not get far away from their guns, remembering how treacherously they had been dealt with in the past.

It was 1892 and Grover Cleveland was running for president of the United States. Election day was bright and clear and all of the Coe Tribe over twenty-one went to the voting-place to cast their ballots. All were cheerful and happy and no one even dreamed of trouble, for all still wanted peace. But quite soon the light was changed to darkness and hostilities had been renewed between the Coe Colony and their old enemies, the Taylors. As was true in the beginning of the strife, the white folks were the aggressors and the instigators of the trouble.

According to the story told by those who were there, Calvin Coe went in, voted, came out and waited for John to follow his example. John went in and, on coming out began looking for Calvin. "Old John" was standing at the entrance waiting an opportunity to enter the voting-place. Shortly after John came out a shot was fired. His first thought was to rush off in the direction from which the sound came, because that had been their agreement when they talked of such eventualities: and now John must put this agreement into effect. John learned afterward, that George Taylor had slipped up behind Calvin Coe and pulling a thirty-eight calibre pistol had begun firing at him without the least warning. One shot struck him at the base of the skull, ranged upward and sped on its way without doing great injury. Another bullet entered the fleshy part of his neck, ranged downward, shattering a banjo which he was carrying under his arm; and, as Calvin was falling to the ground, George Taylor was rushing toward him, still shooting. Witnesses said that as Cal fell, George Taylor was heard to say, "Oh, yes; you yellow dog, I've been after you a long time, and now I got you."

Just as Taylor was uttering these words of vengeance and triumph, the two Johns came rushing up and saw what he had done. They saw Calvin falling to the ground; saw smoke and fire coming from Taylor's gun; and they were like mad men when they saw these things. Thomas Wilburn testified that the two Johns ran up on each side of Taylor and were shooting so that it looked like certain death to go near them. It would have been difficult to tell just how the trouble began, just who fired the first shot, but a few minutes after Taylor had begun the trouble, he was dead, making the second of the Taylors to die in a fight with the Coes. And he had been killed in protection of other lives, just as Will Taylor had been killed.

Another version is that when Little John ran up and saw what was going on he seemed to have become crazed by the sight. He went running toward Taylor and firing his Winchester as he ran. When he was hit by the first shot Taylor turned and tried to run, but did not run far before he fell, pierced by bullets from the two guns. So frenzied were these two men that first the young man and then the old man hit Taylor with their guns, and so hard was the lick which the younger man hit him on the head that the gun with which he hit him was bent almost double.

Looking down on the writhing, struggling body of the foe they had been compelled to kill, "Old John" cried, "God blame it, he ain't dead!" Then, placing his gun against the head of the prostrate man, he fired another shot which entered his brain; but that last, unnecessary shot proved very expensive, as events which follow will substantiate, for it figured very largely in the trial and the sentence of the old man.

After the younger John had struck Taylor the awful blow with the barrel of his gun, as he turned to go to the relief of Calvin, he noticed that his gun was bent. To conceal this he put it under his arm, and swinging it back and forth cried excitedly, "Stand back from me; don't nobody come near; I'll kill you if you do." Reaching Calvin, John asked him if he had any shells. Just about that time some one from the crowd called to him saying, "Your gun is bent; what can you do?" Picking up Calvin's gun he answered, "I have another one just as good, and I'll use it, too, if I have to." "Hold up your gun, John, we are your friends and we want to see how badly Calvin is hurt," came from one of the men nearby; and John agreed, if they would come one at a time, which they did.

When Calvin Coe regained consciousness and found himself lying on the ground with the others grouped around him he asked a number of questions which were answered generally by John Coe, his comrade and inseparable friend. The gist of the questions and answers were:

"What is the matter; and what does all this mean?"
"You have been shot."
"Who shot me?"
"George Taylor."
"Where is George Taylor?"
"We landed him in hell; he is dead."
"Are you sure he is dead?"
"Yes, indeed!"
"All right then; 'cause if he isn't dead I want to kill him."

    It was thus that the wounded man learned that his bitter enemy who had tried to end his life had paid for his effort with his own life, and that one more of the enemies of the Coe Colony had joined the ranks of those who could no longer do anybody harm. But, in his heart, he was sorry it had to be, as he had been sorry that he had to kill Will Taylor, the heartless bully.

    After shooting George Taylor thru the head, "Old John" went to where Calvin Coe lay bleeding, and, with his coat dropped down from his shoulders he stalked back and forth in a challenge to the crowd, shouting, "Where is Taylor's friends? Who'll take up his fight! I ain't got but one time to die and just as soon die now as any other time, come on out you brave men and we'll send you on where George Taylor has gone, to hell!"

    No voice was raised in defense of the dead man. Either because of fear, or because they knew his fate was just, no one made any effort to justify him or to condemn those who had brought his eventful life to a close. When the old man had finished and no one had accepted the challenge, all were surprised to hear one of the men, supposed to be an enemy, offer the use of his horse for Calvin Coe to ride home, since he was too weak to walk. This offer was accepted because of necessity and because the men were as usual, willing to accept any evidence of friendship and any effort toward peace.

There was great excitement when the two Johns arrived at the home of Patsy Ann with Calvin wounded, weak, and bleeding greatly. It was Mandy Coe who screamed, "What is happened now, chillun?" And it was the younger John who answered, "Nothing serious, mother: George Taylor shot Calvin but he will be all right, soon." He continued, "We had to do it; we had to kill him; I bent my gun on his head and he won't ever give nobody no more trouble."

News of the killing was carried by Mandy Coe to the home of Luzette, where she told to the best of her knowledge all that had happened. Being weak and exhausted she sent the news on by her daughter and her niece who ran rapidly to the home of Bill Coe. The writer, a boy of thirteen years, was called by his sister, "Samuel, come here; something terrible has happened!" When I asked what it was my sister blurted out, "Why hell is afloat and the devil can't swim; George Taylor shot Calvin twice; scraped his neck and scraped his head; and Little John shot Taylor six times and "Old John" helped to kill him." Thus came to us at the home of Bill Coe information of the latest tragedy growing out of the feud which it seemed must go on until there could be found some means by which to secure and maintain peace between the Coe Colony and their malicious enemies who constantly and maliciously plotted their destruction, in spite of the fact that they so greatly desired peace with the people among whom they lived.

At Luzette's house, mother was lying on the ground, apparently unable to rise, and when some of the children said, "Get up mother," she groaned deeply and said, "Well, I will, if I can, but this trouble is so heavy; I'm sorry to my heart. I never thought my son would have to kill a man to save his uncle's life, but it seems that was the only way." She added sorrowfully, "Perhaps it is best and if we cannot gain love and friendship by kindness we may gain peace by war." "But it is a terrible thing," was her closing words, as she groaned again.

While all knew that Taylor was wrong in his treacherous attack on Calvin, and that the men were right when they killed him, under such circumstances, yet they feared violence from the Taylor gang and their sympathizers; but the night passed without further trouble, and, in the morning the two Johns surrendered themselves to the law and were put into jail to await the preliminary examination. At the preliminary examination both were bound over to await action of the grand jury. At the first trial, or examination, the younger John was released but the older man was held for trial on the charge of murder.

When "Old John's" trial was held he was accused of committing a felony. The judge told the jury that a man had the right to kill a man who is trying to kill him or who is trying to take the life of another; that such killing is not murder but justifiable homicide. He instructed them if they believed this to be the case, that George Taylor was killed under such circumstances it would be their duty to bring in a verdict of acquittal. But he further instructed that to shoot a man after he was dead was a felony according to general interpretation, and if they believed, from the testimony and evidence, that the accused did shoot George Taylor after he was down, and dead, they should bring in a verdict accordingly.

After half an hour's deliberation the jury returned a verdict of guilty, according to instruction of the court; and the judge gave him a sentence of three years in the state prison, where he must suffer hardships, abuse, and all kinds of humiliation, in spite of the fact that he took a life to save a life — the life of a man who was doing no harm to the one who sought his life.

On his way to trial, the younger John had said to me, a young brother, "Samuel, I am going to trial, and because I was justifiable in what I did I do not expect any trouble, yet, some mean enemy may seek my life, but, if I am killed I want you to hide in the fence corner, with your gun, and shoot every one who have had a part in killing me." A boy of thirteen years, the thought of murder was a terrible thing to me. All of these things ran thru my mind as we went on our way to the court where my brother was to be tried for his life. It was great relief to know that my brother had been set free instead of being sent to prison, but I think the thing that gave me the greatest joy was that no one sought to harm him and I had not been called upon to kill anybody. From that time during the next two years there was peace in the Colony, and it was the most ardent hope of all that peace had come to stay.

CHAPTER ELEVEN
"THE YOUNGER GENERATION"

In the Colony, at the time of the events of this part of the story, were many young men of the adolescent age, and no small number of them were nearing majority. The older people, watching the trend of the minds and the lives of these youths were very much concerned about the future of the Colony, when its affairs must be committed to these young people. While these older ones had been courageous and brave in the defense of their lives and the interests in general, they were lovers of peace and, for the most part conservative in their attitude and activities.

These founders of the Coe Colony were insistent on their rights, but, at the same time, they were modest in their demands, reasonable in their contentions, and willing to make compromise in the interest of peace. More than this, they were temperate in habits, manifestly industrious, honest and truthful, and, for the most part, honest and upright in life and conduct. Considering these facts it should not seem strange that they were somewhat apprehensive in regard to the prosperity and well-being of the community which they had established and which they had made so many sacrifices to improve and advance.

A large number of the boys of the Colony who were just developing into manhood manifested a tendency toward laxness in conduct. Drinking, gambling, indolence and improvidence were prevalent. There was lack of the sterling integrity, rugged honesty and staunch dependability, characteristic of the lives of the older ones. It was this drift from things fundamentally and substantially good that caused alarm among the sires of these young scions of the illustrious Coe Colony.

Another alarming feature was the growing spirit of hatred toward the people of the dominant group whose friendship and goodwill were of such sterling value to those who, by force of circumstances were on an inferior social and political plane. But these youngsters were inclined toward resentment and retaliation. The older ones were moderate and conservative even in contending for and in defending their rights, but these younger ones were inclined to be radical, blatant, and intolerant. The older citizens went to the extreme in defending themselves and their interests only when all pacific methods had failed; but their children were "armed and ready" and often were the aggressors in personal encounters.

One of the lamentable results of this trend and the subsequent alienation of friendship and sympathy was that many of those of the subordinate group were denied employment and were thus forced into indolence, idleness, and thus were given excuse for criminal activities. Departure from moral standards and violation of the law were prevalent and prominent among these young people, and it required no prophet to foretell that direful would be the consequences. And these tendencies, individual and aggregate, were responsible for the apprehension, for the perpetuity and prosperity of the Colony.

One of the first of these younger ones to get into serious trouble as the result of his own mistake was Joseph Coe, eighteen, son of

Thomas Coe and grandson of Ezekiel Coe. Joseph considered himself old enough to take care of himself and to make his own contracts for employment. Accordingly he entered into a verbal contract with one, Bill Williams, to move some logs, thinking that this would be equal to a written contract. This man Williams repudiated the contract, had Joseph arrested, and, as the logs were in Clay County, Tennessee, he was tried in that county and sentenced to one year in the penitentiary at Nashville and leased to a farmer for whom he served the entire term of his sentence.

In the case of Joseph Coe and the direful consequences of the injustice done him we have a forceful illustration of the nefarious convict-leasing system of the southern states. This system began just after the Civil War; it was used to take advantage of ignorant and helpless freedmen; tho profitable to the state, it was degrading and unjust to those on whom it was practiced; and, because of the profit it extended to practically every southern state and has survived until this very day. It also might be added that finally it came to the point where white men were victims as well as those of the darker hue.

This system is unfair, unjust, and is subversive of the real purpose of our judiciary and penal system, which, properly applied would be benevolently corrective rather than vindictively punitive. The State is supposed to punish in the interest of society; for the purpose of preventing crime and improving social conditions. But when prisoners are leased to unprincipled men who exploit them, the State itself condones and encourages crime and so contradicts its own theories and counteracts all of the utilitarianism possible from the punishment of crime.

Again, this system is unfair to laboring men and the employers of free labor, for neither the laborer nor the employer of free labor can compete with the cheap labor afforded by the leasing system. This handicaps industry, works economic hardships, results in idleness, and, to no small extent results in more crime. It was true during the stirring days of this period, and the same effects are in evidence today.

Celina, Tennessee, at the point where the Obey River emptied into the Cumberland River was one of the prominent log centers, therefore, when the water was high, the boys from the Pea Ridge settlement would go there seeking employment, moving logs in rafts, down the Cumberland River to Nashville. As a matter of adventure, three boys of the Coe Tribe, Jesse Coe, Robert Coe, and Sherly Wilburn went to this place for the purpose of having a ride down the river, as well as for the money they would make. Shortly after their arrival, while standing in a store, Jesse Coe was accosted by a man who was to him an entire stranger, and who asked abruptly, "Ain't you that banjer player?" Quietly he answered, "I am not a banjo player, but I try to play a banjo sometimes." The other man demanded to know what he was "rattling" in his pocket, and before he could answer, this ruffian struck him, pushed him, and giving a terrific kick, sent him sprawling out thru the back door to the ground ten feet below.

Getting up from the ground, tho stunned and dazed by the licks and the fall, this boy made his way back to the front of the store, and climbing over a high fence entered the store again, passing thru a crowd of excited men. When the storekeeper saw him he said in frightened tones, "You better go away from here; you goin' to git plenty trouble on yor hands." This Jesse did not understand, because the man was a stranger and he had done nothing to him. The man still urged, telling him, "If you start anything here you have the whole town to fight." He refused to go, demanding to know who was the man that struck him and for what.

"I'm the man what struck you and I'm the man what will kill you," came from outside the store, and all knew that it meant serious trouble. Jesse made his way to the front door, saw this man with his gun raised, and at one time he thought to run, as he had nothing to defend himself with but a knife. He remembered that Coes were never cowards. He thought of his Uncle Calvin who had pleaded with Will Taylor for peace and then had to kill him. Then came to his mind that

Oleson Wilburn had been murdered while begging for his life and with nothing to defend his life with. He remembered too, that his Uncle Joe had been shot by George Taylor and without even an opportunity to plead for his life; and with all this in his mind Jesse was certain it would be useless to plead with the man who had decided to injure him, and perhaps kill him, for no cause whatsoever. He knew that either he must defend himself or he must die without mercy.

While these thoughts were surging thru his mind, the gun was fired and a bullet crashed into his side, stunning him and making him furious. In an instant, he sprang over the steps of the store and upon his enemy, and they entered into a life and death struggle. The force of the contact sent the man to the ground with Jesse on top of him. He got a hold of the gun of the murderer; they continued to struggle for its possession; Jesse turned the gun from him and toward the other man, pulled the trigger, and the shot went into his side. He released the gun and was turning to run when Jesse sent another bullet into his side and then one into his back. The man staggered to a tree, leaned against it, and then slowly slipped down to the ground — and in a few minutes was dead.

Of those who stood by, one man, a fellow named Bowman interfered. He seized a rock and cried, "My blood is jest briling for you," but when he saw the pistol in Jesse's hand pointing toward him he dropped his rock and hurried away. Amid the excitement a deputy sheriff came up, rushed to Jesse and informed him that the man he shot was Milt Williams and that he was dead. Jesse was growing weak from loss of blood and made no resistance when the deputy declared him under arrest and demanded his gun. When he told the officer, "I am shot; I am weak and cannot walk to jail," his reply was, "That ain't none of my business; you killed a man and you got to go to jail." But he did call some of the men nearby to come and take the wounded man to the jail.

The crowd was angry and threatening and it seemed that they

would form a mob and seek the life of the prisoner. The men who were carrying him were afraid and began to rush with him. But, with the usual courage of the unconquerable Coes, he said, "You don't have to run with me; if they come just give me a gun and I'll swap it out with 'em." But the mob did not form; they were not molested; Jesse was landed in jail; and the other boys escaped and made their way back to the Colony to tell of the latest misfortune to overtake one of the Colony, arriving at headquarters about midnight.

Because he had always taken an active part in defending the members of the Colony and because he was considered the leader of all, the boys went first to the home of John Coe, who noting their excitement asked, "Well, boys, what has happened now?" One explained very bluntly, "We come to tell you your brother Jesse got shot this afternoon, at Celina; but we think it ain't very serious." After he had listened to the explanation, Johnny sent out a general alarm, and when his voice rang out on the night air, members of the tribe went rushing, for they knew that was a signal that there was trouble or danger somewhere.

An inventory revealed that the Colony was short on ammunition and all knew that they did not dare to go to Celina without a full supply, so they elected Thomas E. Coe to go fifteen miles to Tompkinsville for a full supply, and sent Hance Williams to ferry him across the river, knowing that the ferryman would be asleep. As might have been known, all the stores were closed and Thomas was compelled to wait until the next morning to make the purchase.

On his way back he was surprised to have a white man ask him in what part of the body Jesse was shot. He was also surprised to learn that from Tompkinsville some one had telephoned to Celina saying, "Be careful down there; the Coe boys have been here and bought a sack of ammunition and will soon be there to make trouble. Arriving about noon Thomas found the men of the tribe anxiously awaiting his return and fully ready to start to Celina. He found also that Mandy, Jesse's mother, and Ada, his sister had left early in the morning for Celina, to see what could be done for Jesse.

Now armed and prepared for whatever might come, the Coe army started on the march to Celina, determined to protect one of their own at whatever cost might be required, for they were never known to desert one another in time of trouble or of danger. They were peaceable and law-abiding, but when violence was attempted and injustice done they would meet violence with violence. They realized that this must be done; that their enemies must be made to fear them and thus avoid trouble with them, or they would be wiped off the face of the earth.

On their way they had a parley with a man named Bill Murley. This man was friendly toward all the people; he believed in justice and fair play; in any controversy he would speak to those on both sides and try to effect a compromise and avoid serious trouble; and when he heard that the Coes were armed and marching toward Celina he knew it meant bloodshed. For this reason he quickly mounted his horse and overtook them before they had gone very far on their journey. He informed them that he had been to Celina that very morning and that Jesse was in no danger.

The chief mission of Mr. Murley was to persuade the Coes from going to Celina, and that was largely because he knew what would happen to them. He told them of the message that had gone from Tompkinsville about the bag of ammunition; he informed them of the spirit of the people down there and that all was in readiness to meet them; he argued with them that the people would have advantage in that they could and would hide in the various buildings and shoot from their hiding places; and, as a friend he begged them to remain at home and let the law take its course. It was Calvin Coe, the man who had been so often in danger and had so many narrow escapes who said hotly, "Well, Mr. Murley, your intentions may be good, and I cannot say what the others will do, but I am going to Celina!" That ended the parley; they started again on the way, and the peace-maker turned away with a sad countenance, and with a heavy heart.

They had not gone far before they met Mandy, and Ada, the mother and sister of Jesse, on their way back from Celina, and the mother told them that she had been there, had seen Jesse, that he was in no danger and in good spirits; and she urged the boys not to go lest it would cause very serious trouble and more killing. They hesitated, and the first to speak was John Coe, who said with great emphasis, "I am ready to protect our own; I am willing to fight and die, if need be; but I don't want to kill nobody if I can help it, so, since mother says Jesse is all right, I am going back home and allow the law to have its course." And the Coe army retreated, returning to their homes to await further developments. Jesse Coe was tried, convicted and sent to prison for three years, despite the fact that he was defending his own life. But such was and such is the miscarriage of justice when and where men see through their prejudices rather than thru their eyes; where the color of a man's skin counts more than the cultivation of his intellect and the honesty of his heart. Such it was; such it is today; and such it will be until enlightenment and altruism shall succeed in the elevation of justice to the throne, in America — and throughout the world.

Considering conditions at the time of this story and that until this day this reckless, unreasoning prejudice and its resultant palpable injustice are holding sway, one is forced to marvel at the loyalty of those on whom these things are so ruthlessly practiced. How they can continue to love the nation which denies them their "inalienable rights" and oppresses them on every hand is indeed an enigma. That they can love the flag that will essay to protect its humblest citizen anywhere in the wide world and yet allow those who are among its most loyal citizens to be mobbed, mutilated, dismembered, and incinerated adds to the already seemingly insoluble mystery.

Here is one version expressed by one of the poets of these people:

This is my flag!
Although this seemth not to be
"Home of the brave; land of the free,"
Yet, loyally, I honor thee,
    My nation's flag.

Thou art my flag!
Although within thy very sight,
Wrong often triumphs over Right,
I'll wait the dawning of the light,
    For thee, my flag!

Thou art my flag!
Mine are the red, the white, the blue,
Mine are the stars — and the STRIPES, too,
And, unto thee I will be true,
    My Country's flag!

Thou art my flag!
And may God haste the day
When Wrong shall die, and Right hold sway,
And none shall be ashamed to say —
    This is my FLAG!

CHAPTER TWELVE
HIGH LIGHTS AND DEEP SHADOWS

Down at Celina it was decided to try the other boys who were with Jesse Coe, when he killed Milt Williams, those it was generally known that they took no part in the affair, not even when the men were in their life and death struggle. But, since the killing was in Clay County, Tennessee, and these boys were in Kentucky, the problem was to get them back to Celina for trial. They knew that unless they would be willing to return, there was no other way than to secure requisition papers from the governor of Kentucky, a course of procedure they did not want to take. This matter was one of great concern to the officer whose duty it was to secure the accused boys and present them for trial in Celina.

Since the killing, there had been an election in Clay County, Tennessee, and a man named Joe Parker had been elected sheriff. He was a good man, and while he was brave and daring he did not want bloodshed were it could be avoided, so he thought of a way to get the boys back without serious trouble. A man named Sam Hance was sent to persuade the boys to surrender and go back to Celina without getting the papers from the governor, and he enlisted assistance from that lover of peace, Bill Murley. He was glad to go, because he wanted to prevent what he knew would happen if they attempted to take the boys without their consent.

The council was held at the home of Thomas Wilburn and both the deputy and Mr. Murley sought to persuade the boys to return voluntarily. Murley was frank enough to say that he was confident that they were guilty of no crime; that, under the circumstances he would have done just what they did; that he would use all his influence to see to it that no violence would be done to them on the way, and that they should have a fair trial. He urged, "Boys, they want you to go down there and it is best to go because their guns are in your face." With utmost composure, Sherly said, "Mr. Murley, we are not thinking of the guns for we have had guns in our faces many times; but we are afraid we will not get justice and that we may be punished for crimes we have not committed."

Both the officer and Murley pledged that no harm should be done them on the way; that they would protect them to the very last; and that they would do their best in the matter of a fair trial; and finally the boys consented to go, because of these promises and because they knew they were innocent of any crime. With his face giving evidence of the tenseness of his feelings and his tones expressive of his determination to do all that he was saying, Thomas Wilburn looked at Murley and said, "Mr. Murley these boys do not have to go back unless they want to; we would never permit them to be carried back against their will; they have agreed to go with you, because we all have confidence in you; and we are expecting you to protect them from mob violence, as you have promised, and if they are injured in any way, we will hold you responsible; and Mr. Murley, if they are murdered, you cannot stay in the flesh!" He accepted the responsibility and soon they were on their way to Celina.

Fearing that the prisoners could not get a fair trial in Celina because of the bitter feeling against them, Joe Parker decided that it would be better to have them get what is called a "change of venue" and have their trial in Livingston. In connection with this change a very strange and surprising thing happened, namely, the sheriff requested the assistance of John Coe in conveying the prisoners to Livingston. This was exceptionally strange for the reason that John lived in Kentucky and the proceedings were held in Tennessee. But the suspicion was that the sheriff wanted to be sure they would reach Livingston, and knowing the bravery of John, and that he would fight for his own to the very end, he considered the help of John as a deputy to be the very best assurance of success in what he knew to be a perilous task. He knew too, that few men who knew anything of the Coes would risk their lives to the extent of interfering if John Coe was there with his gun.

John was surprised and puzzled. One feature which gave him great concern was the fact that the sheriff advised him that he need not bring his gun, for he would supply him with a gun and ample ammunition. Some of them feared that this might be a plan to catch John unarmed and do him violence; but others argued that no man who knew would take chances with his life, knowing that the Coes would most certainly avenge the death of John, if he should be injured. It was finally decided to trust the sheriff and let John go, since it accorded opportunity to protect the innocent boys who were to be tried.

John Coe, the deputy sheriff, tells a strange story but a very interesting one about the trip from Celina to Livingston, but only the high-lights will be given here, for no one could tell the story as he could. As a precaution, the sheriff had with him three other deputies, and tho they were officers of the law and supposed to be sober and sane, they had an ample supply of whiskey with them. It seems that one of the deputies, a Millard Kyle was the heaviest drinker and the first to get an over-supply on the inside. Full to the brim, John said this deputy began to fire his gun very rapidly, tho aimlessly, and he became rebellious and troublesome when the sheriff ordered him to give up the gun, which he refused to do.

According to the story, the sheriff seized the drunken deputy and attempted to take the gun from him. They struggled terrifically but he was too strong for the sheriff to disarm him. It was then that the sheriff called to the other deputies to get their guns ready to shoot the drunken one. But, before he would give up the gun he threw it into a stream of water near, then threatened to whip the whole crowd without a gun. They reached Livingston where the two boys were placed in jail, and when they entered they found Jesse playing on his banjo and singing some of the old Kentucky songs, as if nothing had happened.

When the trial was held, Jesse was found guilty and given a prison sentence of two years, and the other boys were acquitted and immediately left for their home, sad to leave Jesse, but glad they had escaped the injustice which was meted out to him. Jesse was soon carried away to Nashville where he served out his sentence in full.

It might truthfully be said that in sending old man John to prison for his part in the killing of the desperado, George Taylor, in dealing severely with Joseph Coe for what at best was a mistake caused by over confidence of youth, then, in giving Jesse Coe this sentence of two years for killing in self defense, and after the attempt to take his life, we have again an illustration of that strange, cruel, malevolent, unrelenting and destructive thing called racial prejudice, as it is manifest in our judiciary proceedings and in our penal operations.

In the Coe Colony they were eagerly awaiting news from Livingston, and when the boys returned the people had a sense of joy mingled with sorrow. They were glad that the two boys had escaped the unjust punishment they feared, such as came to Jesse, but they were sorry Jesse had to be punished so severely when in all that he did he was defending his own life. But they had decided to let the law take its course, so they bowed their heads and accepted the results, hoping that that would be the end of strife and suffering among them.

Almost a year had passed with no special calamity to disturb the trend of things when suddenly they experienced deep sorrow caused by the sudden death of Billy Wilburn, an ambitious and courageous fellow who was drowned under suspicious circumstances. This was surprising and suspicious because Billy was known to be an excellent swimmer and it was difficult to convince the people that there had not been foul play, somehow. A young man who was in the skiff with him said looking back he saw Billy stand up in his end of the skiff and then fall backward into the water. He tried to catch him but he went down and came up rapidly, and finally he failed to rise again. The water was thirty feet deep where he went down, and tho the search for Billy's body continued three days, it was not located until a young man from Martinburg went out in a skiff and soon located it.

In the discussion of his death it came out that Billy was subject to some kind of spells; that they seized him just anywhere; and at the time he would be affected by a spell this was his custom to stand up and fall backward just as the young man had described his actions on the day he was drowned. After this fact had been established, suspicion of foul play was ended and the accident theory fully accepted. Billy was the second son of Mary Wilburn to die an untimely death and it seemed that she would give way under this new load of sorrow. Her grief was so deep that her husband, Thomas Wilburn, a man not easily moved entered deeply into sympathy with her and sought in every way to comfort her.

In 1896 "Old John" came home, after serving sentence of three years for his part in the killing of George Taylor. He was a changed man. His back was bent, his hair was white and his countenance sad. He looked to be ten years older than when he was sent to prison three years before. The old man greeted his friends, and shaking his head dolefully said, "I have carried my gun to protect my friends; I'll do it again, if I must; but I am tired of confusion and strife and would be glad if I could put the gun aside and never see it again, for I am tired of fighting." Old John was sincere. He wanted peace, peace among themselves and peace with their neighbors!

In 1898, two years after the return of "Old John," Jesse Coe came home from the state prison at Nashville, and, as he reached the Colony began to yell like a wild Indian. He cried out as loudly as he could, "Can't you hear me, old home; I am back again!" The writer, Jesse's brother and his two sisters went out to meet him and others followed, glad to give Jesse a welcome back home, after all that he had suffered. But they found him a different person. In his conduct was the evidence of the influence of his association with the wicked men at the prison in Nashville; and this discovery made them sad.

Jesse had come out of prison with a grudge against the world. He seemed bent on getting even with everybody that ever did anything to him or to his people. He was ready to resent everything that seemed like ill feeling toward him. He was always ready for a fight and seemed to think that everyone except his own folks were against him. This attitude the members of the Coe Colony deplored, for they knew it meant not only trouble for him but for them all, since they must not and would not forsake him in time of trouble. The people of the community knew the circumstances, sympathized with the foolish fellow and avoided any trouble with him.

One of the most lamentable cases in the annals of the Coe Tribe was that of Sherman Wilburn, born in 1876, a poor boy who was more deserving of pity than of condemnation. No doubt his parents tried to teach him what was right and to train him to do what was right. But these people were themselves born in slavery when they learned but little more than obedience to their master, knew but little to teach their children, except that which they knew by intuition; but they knew enough to know that the only way to safety is the right way, and that they tried to instill within their children. They gave special attention to Sherman who was the most incorrigible and the heedless of all.

One day while in school, Sherman became unruly and the teacher attempted to correct him. According to the story, he fought like a tiger, but the teacher was stronger and subdued him at that time. Soon this boy left school, went home and seized his brother's gun and went back to kill the teacher. He called him out, challenged him for a finished fight, then dared him to show his head, threatening to shoot him if he did. When he could not get the teacher out he returned home, put up the gun and went to a moon-shiner's camp and spent four days. Returning, his father punished him severely, and for this reason he again ran away and was gone quite a while before they found his hiding place.

At a log camp, Sherman became angry and abusive to a man who was betting on a game in which he was engaged and even refused to listen to his uncle Calvin who tried to prevail with him to desist from such a dangerous practice. The day after the man was there with a gun ready to kill Sherman and but for the fact that the other Coes were there and ran to his rescue his life would have ended then and there. But this poor, foolish abusive fellow tried his folly once too often and came to an untimely end, as was generally expected, even long before it happened.

This rough, overbearing fellow was working for a big, rough red-faced man named Vincent Vaughn, a man who had his own ideas about righteousness and morality, and Sherman Wilburn and Vince Vaughn were constantly having trouble between them. At one time they had a personal conflict, both fighting with their fists; this was the beginning of the end for Sherman. At the home of Patsy Ann, his grandmother, he was handling a little pistol known as a "41," when "Old John" warned, "You better throw that thing behind the fire, now, cause in a fight it will fail you and get you killed." But the bully simply laughed at this warning and went on his way.

Some months later Sherman agreed to pilot a raft of logs down the Cumberland River, for Vince Vaughn, but before they were ready they had more trouble and there were more threats. At this time Sherman abused Vaughn as before. The next day, while talking to his sweetheart, a Miss McMullen, his brother Garfield informed him that Vaughn had sent for him, saying he wanted him to take the logs to Nashville as they first had agreed. With regrets he left and went to the camp where he found Vaughn waiting for him and apparently in a good humor.

"Well, Mr. Vaughn, you have changed your mind, have you," was the greeting from Sherman. "Yes," answered Vaughn, "I got nothin' against you; I'll treat you right if you will stop your bad language and do right." Instead of meeting Mr. Vaughn in the same spirit, Sherman replied, "I like your work; but, Vince Vaughn, you must not talk to me like you been talking or else one of us will be put away for keeps." It seems that Vaughn had decided to provoke Sherman and make him say rough things that he might have an excuse to kill him; and it worked well.

Thoroughly angry now, Sherman fairly shouted, "You know I'm a free man, and I never allow any man to say more to me than I say to him, and if nothin' else will do we will settle our trouble right now, and for all time!" As he spoke Sherman pulled his little gun and fired it at Mr. Vaughn, missing him. Vaughn quickly drew his "45," fired twice at Sherman, hitting him both times. The first shot hit him in the breast and the last one struck him in the neck, just as he was falling. He lived just twenty-four hours and passed into the great beyond, dying as he did as a victim of his own consummate folly.

Fearing the vengeance of the Coes, Vaughn left the settlement and remained away in hiding for six months. But he was in no danger. The Tribe held council, as was their custom, went over the facts in the case, were convinced that Sherman was in fault and that Vaughn shot to save his life, as did Calvin Coe, John Coe, Jesse Coe, and others, and they decided that it would be unjust to molest Vaughn for protecting his own life as they would have done, under such circumstances. When Vaughn knew they would not hurt him, he came out of hiding, surrendered himself, was tried and acquitted and lived in the community without being molested.

CHAPTER THIRTEEN
REAPING THE WHIRLWIND

———◆▸✕◂◆———

In a previous chapter a few things were recorded concerning Joseph Coe, the young man who got into trouble thru a mistake caused by the unfounded self-confidence of youth and as the result served one year in the State prison at Nashville. It has been noted that he came out of prison calloused, intemperate, revengeful, and recklessly wicked, as result of evil associations during his period of penal servitude. During the first three years after his return from prison, Joseph, in the mountains of Kentucky, was notoriously wicked; and yet, to the time of this story he had never killed a man.

As an example of the variableness of this young fellow, he married twice in two years but did not live long with either wife. In other things he was as in this particular liable to change suddenly, without any cause. He was a restless wanderer who seemed never satisfied. Because of his wickedness and his instability he was generally feared. Tho he had not killed anyone, he carried his gun and everybody was certain that he would shoot if sufficient provocation should be given. But, like others of this kind, this boy was a creature of circumstances, and the good qualities found in him indicated that with different environment and better opportunities he would have been a different and a better man.

This young man seemed to have lost all care for himself and all fear of consequences. He thought of what the others of the Colony had done for themselves and their friends and seemed to have reached the conclusion that the name Coe would move mountains. In this weakness of self-inflation he seemed to have some of the spirit of the Taylor brothers who thought their name was sufficient to inspire fear and awe everywhere. Joseph thought that because of what he considered himself to be, others must take orders from him and that he had the right to decide not only his own conduct but the conduct of others as well. And it was this spirit of self importance, his disposition to domineer that made trouble for him and proved his undoing. To him and his conduct might aptly be applied the maxim, "A wise man thinks of what is just; but nothing matters, to a fool."

On Christmas Eve morning, 1900, while the children at the home of Bill Coe were playing around their Christmas tree, a man came in hastily and said, "Joseph Coe got shot today, but nobody knows how serious it is; and that broke up the preparation for Christmas celebration. Joseph lived ten miles away, and the older members rushed there as rapidly as possible. As Joseph told the story, he was drinking but was not drunk; he was standing near a store sporting with his horse, making him "turn around on a nickel;" for no special reason he fired his gun twice, aiming at nothing. At this time, he claims that two men came to him, stood one on each side of him, and began firing their guns at him, and all of this without the least explanation. After they had shot at him they ran away as fast as possible with Joseph in hot pursuit.

When Joseph overtook one of the men, Joseph Cloyd, this fellow denied shooting at him. He could not determine, because both seemed to be shooting and he could not tell which shot first not which one hit him. Joseph admits that he tried to shoot this man and his gun failed to fire. The other had a thirty-two Winchester, and taking shelter behind an old chimney, he shot Joseph in the face, paralyzing his jaw, and after this he ran away. Of the man Joseph said, "I knew he was a bad man; that he had killed a man; that he always had his gun; that he had served a term in the penitentiary; yet I was not afraid of him, and if my gun had not failed me, I would have left him right there." His wound was slight and he soon recovered.

The day after Joseph was shot a number the tribe went to the store where he had the fight. As they came to the front a man was seen running from the rear, and Joseph raised his gun to shoot, when Calvin Coe, the man who was brave and yet an advocate of peace quickly grabbed his gun and prevented him from the hasty deed. The peacemaker said, "We are not here to make trouble; but to make peace, if we can. We didn't come to start a mob, for our purpose is to put down mobs." His counsel prevailed and they went home without serious trouble, all glad that no blood had been shed.

Not long after this occurrence Joseph had trouble with a man named Bedford Hill. He was out of money, out of work and out of provisions, and went to Mr. Hill and asked to supply him with provisions until he could secure work. He offered to work for Hill and pay for anything he might buy on credit. Mr. Hill seemed unconcerned and flatly refused him. Angry, Joseph turned away saying, "I've tried to be a gentleman; I have nothing to eat and I am willing to work for provisions; now if I cannot get what I need by fair means I will by foul means." And he went immediately and stole one of the old man's hogs and sold it.

When Hill took him to task about his hog he denied it, and he cursed and abused the old man to a great extent, and said to him, "I'll see you again and we will settle the whole matter once for all." A little later he passed by where Bedford Hill was threshing wheat, and again he cursed him and abused him. Hill ran in, got his gun and came running out, but, somehow when he saw Joseph's gun pointed toward him he became excited and dropped to the ground, apparently overcome by fright. Joseph refused to shoot him lying on the ground, and thus the matter ended.

There was not further trouble between Joseph and Bedford, because of the fact that the former soon moved to Indianapolis, Indiana, changed his name to Bob Porter, and lived there twenty-five years, and then died in one of the hospitals from the effects of drinking poisoned alcohol.

CHAPTER FOURTEEN
A MOTHER'S BROKEN HEART

In the interest of fair play, it is necessary to say a few words concerning Mr. Bedford Hill, the man who ran Joseph Coe away from the Colony and from the state. This Mr. Hill was one of the best farmers of the section; he was generous and, as a general thing was always ready to aid anyone really in need. He was prosperous and willing to give work to as many persons as possible, and he was not a difficult man to please; so, in spite of his dealing Joseph Coe, he was not a mean man to work for or to deal with. One other thing about Hill is that he was not too big to confess when he had made a mistake or had done any wrong.

After he had caused Joseph Coe to leave the settlement he telephoned for miles around trying to apprehend him. After he found out that Joseph had gone to Indianapolis he sent a man to Indianapolis thinking to get him back. The officers arrested Jesse Coe, and when they found out the truth, they had the wrong man, they released him. After he failed to get Joseph back, and after he thought over the whole matter and realized that he had been unkind when he refused to give this boy work by which to make a living, his conscience condemned him and he dropped the case against Joseph and allowed him to go on unmolested; and thus the case of Joseph ended and no other efforts were made to take him to Kentucky for trial and punishment.

Another sad and untimely death in the Colony was that of Sherly Wilburn, and which resulted from his disposition to ignore advice and to attempt what was most difficult, if not impossible. He was a good worker, a man who looked after his business and did not interfere with others, but his over-confidence was his undoing. Sherly was the third son of Mary Wilburn and the fourth son to die prematurely. It will be remembered that his brother Oleson was shot to death, August 1889, while on his way to Mud Camp; his next brother Billy was drowned in the Cumberland River, in 1896; the third one, Sherman Wilburn, was shot to death by Vince Vaughn in 1900.

During his boyhood days Sherly would attempt anything, so, one day while he and a number of boys were standing near the river bank he suddenly decided to jump into the water, though he knew nothing about swimming, and there was about thirty feet of water in the channel. The other boys tried to reason with him; they reminded him that he could not swim and of the danger of an undertaking like that; but he made the careless remark, "It won't make any difference; I'll jump in if I die hard." He jumped in and would have drowned but for the fact that some of the boys reached him, in a skiff, just as he was going down the last time. And this spirit, this bull-dog-go-ahead idea caused him to die an untimely death.

In the spring of 1902 a number of the young men of the Colony were taking a raft of logs down the Cumberland River to Nashville, Tennessee. At one point they tied the raft near the bank and endeavored to get a little rest and sleep. They had a good skiff tied to the raft, also they had an old one, which they carried on the raft; and this one became dry and unsafe. During the night, by some means the good skiff got loose, while all were asleep, and it went drifting on down the river. Finding themselves minus their skiff they cut loose the raft and went drifting down. Finally as they began to enter what was known as the King's Eddies, they saw their skiff not far ahead.

Seeing the skiff, Sherly said, "There is our skiff boys, let us use this old one and go and get it." It was Calvin Coe who objected, saying, "This old skiff has been lying here in the sun, is dry, and will leak; it is dangerous to risk it in the water." Laughing at the counsel, Sherly hurried on, dragged the old boat and launched it, but not one of the other boys would get into the boat with him, because all knew how dangerous it was. This brave but foolish fellow urged, but no one would agree. He called on Robert to get in with him, but Robert said, "No; that old boat will go down and I cannot afford to risk it." After a while, and after Sherly had cursed and raved, one of the boys, George Williams got into the skiff with him and they were off.

They had not gone far when the old skiff filled up very rapidly and was sinking. From the raft the boys could see the distress of the two on the skiff but they were powerless to help them, since the water was high and swift, and very cold. Seeing Sherly about to leave the boat in an attempt to swim they called and urged him to hold onto it; but, headstrong as usual he refused to listen. With a .45 calibre pistol buckled on him, and wrapped in a heavy overcoat, it was impossible for him to keep afloat very long, and with all that weight. It was not long before he cried, "Boys, I can't make it," and he sank down to rise no more.

George Williams, who was in the skiff with Sherly said he did not know what to do, but when he heard the boys cry, "Hold on to the boat," he knew that was the only hope; so he held on for his life. After his rescue by some boys who rushed out from the shore he told his story, how the water was cold, his hands were slipping, his strength was almost gone, his body chilled until he almost lost sensation; and he had almost given up the effort. He was taken to a home nearby and in a measure restored. The next morning he got into a skiff and attempted to overtake the boys on the raft, but they had gone on too rapidly, as the river was high and the current swift. They reached Nashville the next morning and George reached there later in the day. One of the saddest features of the fate of Sherly is that his body was never found.

When the news of the drowning of Sherly Wilburn reached the Colony, they could scarcely believe it, for all knew that he was a good swimmer, at that time; then, they had heard such sad stories before, and they had proved to be false. When the boys returned in tears, weeping for their lost comrade, then all knew that report was true, and there was mourning throughout the Colony. When Calvin told the story to his sister, Mary Wilburn, Sherly's mother, she became hysterical. After she sobbed a while she said, "Brother Calvin, I never can forgive you, for I know you could have kept my boy from taking such a risk."

Calvin was not harsh with his sister, knowing how she was grieved over the loss of her son. He answered her mildly, "Well, sister, you know we would have prevented the sad occurrence if we could have done so. We knew the boat was not safe, but did not know positively that it would sink. But we all warned the boy of the danger and urged him not to take the risk, and he refused to listen, determined to have his own way, which he did."

Mary Wilburn began crying afresh, saying between her sobs, "Two of my boys were shot to death; one drowned before this one, and we got him out of the water and saw him decently buried; and I want Sherly's body brought home so I can see it buried like the others." And her brother promised that he would do his best to accomplish her desires. From the Colony he selected two of the boys to make the search. They made the trip down the river, to Nashville, succeeded in having dug up every body that had been drowned and buried along the river bank but they could not find Sherly's body, and had to return home with the sad news of their failure.

The two boys who went in search of Sherly's body were Thomas E. Coe, Mary's son-in-law, and Garfield, her youngest son. Garfield was just recovering from an attack of the measles, when he was sent on this mission, and the cold and the exposure caused relapse, from which he did not recover; and Mary Wilburn had lost her fifth son. This final blow was too much for this woman who had so bravely stood all the sorrows that had come to her, and she soon succumbed, and one of the bravest souls that ever lived passed to her rest.

At this time, out of the six boys of the Wilburn family, there was left only one, Charley, and it seemed that the energy and strength of the family had centered in him, and as the others had been unfortunate, he seemed to be fortunate to as great a degree, for practically everything he put his hands to prospered. He purchased a farm and paid for it in two years. Tho he worked both day and night, he managed to keep it up and retain his health. All of his family members were industrious and helped him on his farm and in everything he attempted to do, and he was prosperous in practically every way.

In his younger days, Charley was a mischievous fellow, but he was not vicious and mean. Before he had a family of his own he was always employed and delighted to do his part in keeping up the interest and the expense of his mother's family. He was as peaceable as he was industrious, tried to help his older brothers who were inclined to be rash and to live in peace with the neighbors on the outside as well as the members of the Colony. He was not a coward, but he loved peace and hated strife and bloodshed of which he had seen so much in the Colony. This man was not only industrious but he was economical, as well, and succeeded in accumulating property; and thus Charley was one of the brightest lights of the entire Coe Colony.

The contrast between his prosperous life and the credit and honor he won and that of his brothers who were unfortunate was very strikingly manifested; and his life of peace and prosperity gave evidence of the superiority of quietness, peace, and conservative living over rashness, recklessness, indifference and surrender to anger and revenge. And it would have been well that those of the "younger generation" had emulated the peace-loving, industrious, conservative spirit of Charley Wilburn. It would have been better for them, and the story of some of their lives would have had a different and less tragic ending. But, such is life and its uncertainties, inequalities — and it's tragedies!

CHAPTER FIFTEEN
TRANSGRESSIONS AND TRAGEDIES

———◆◆◆———

This chapter brings us to the closing career of one of the most unfortunate of the Coe Colony, namely, Jesse Coe, of whose life much of praise and much of blame might be written. Members of the Colony were not proud of the mistakes of Jesse; they got no pleasure out of the tragedies with which he was connected; they regretted the mistakes he made; but they loved him as one of their own, and naturally they were grieved at his untimely and tragic end. And, in this they made allowance for his mistakes, when they thought of certain things which entered into his life and influenced it, to a great extent.

As it will be remembered, Jesse had to kill a man to save himself from being killed, yet he was convicted and forced to serve a sentence for this act in defense of his own life, and the association with criminals had influence on his mind. He felt the sting of injustice in his sentence, and came out with vengeance in his heart and bitterness against those who had dealt unjustly with him. Tired of the persecutions at home, in the year 1901 he left Kentucky and went to Indianapolis, Indiana to live. Being hampered for lack of industrial training he had to seek work of any kind and wherever he could find it, hence, for a good part of his time he was walking the streets seeking employment by which to make an honest living, for still he was willing to work for what he needed for his comfort.

Walking the streets of Indianapolis, seeking work and finding none, the old spirit of revenge and of rebellion against unjust conditions became stronger in his life. He not only resented what was done to him, but resented the injustice done to others because he knew this was a part of the system of injustice existing in this country. Another thing, the mistreatment of this man seemed to have driven him out of his mind, the thought of what may be a man's portion hereafter, for he seemed to think it was the right thing to take care of conditions here and allow the hereafter to take care of itself, which, of course, was a mistaken idea. He hated the race distinctions and the hypocrisy of any man and expressed it in the words, "If any man claims that you can segregate and mistreat members of any division of the human race and still be a Christian, he is a damned liar."

Jesse Coe's hatred was aroused by the conduct of officers of Indianapolis. In regard to some of them, it seemed that they were very low in character and had just decided to get behind their uniform to hide their real character and enable them to do their dirty work. Of course, in this respect the officers of Indianapolis were not different from officers of that class in other cities, but he was brought into contract with these, and he hated them and their ideas of justice. They seemed to forget that tho a man had made some mistakes or had broken some law he was still a human being, and that guilty or not he has certain rights and is entitled to certain consideration even while in the custody of the law; and these things had to do with his attitude toward the officers of the law, and they had to do with the occurrence which caused the end of his life.

In this very city of Indianapolis, in 1902, the writer was attacked by what is known as a "bungelow gang," and a policeman who was near could have stopped the trouble with a word, but he stood there with his hands behind him as if he were a member of the gang or enjoyed watching them at their lawless work. This man is a sample of officers of the law who are sworn to protect people and who failed to do so; and they are deserving of the condemnation and the contempt of all the people. Such officers are a greater help to criminals than they are a protection to the citizens they are sworn to protect.

At another time, in this same city, there was a bunch of boys engaged in a game of dice, called "craps," and when they ran, at the approach of a policeman, this brutal officer fired into the crowd, shot one boy in the eye and caused the loss of that eye, altogether. This boy who was one of our Kentucky boys, ran, as did the others, thinking they might escape the officer. They did not think that he was a man who would be heartless enough to kill a man and become a murderer just to hear his own gun fire! They had no idea that his man, wearing the uniform of an officer of the law could kill anyone he might choose and "get away with it." But, this brutal man was just that kind, and when the boys began to run, and did not stop when he called them to halt, he fired at them and caused this boy to lose the use of his eye.

Jesse Coe knew of these two instances of injustice and he became more bitter against the policemen of the city and decided wrongly, of course, that he was not entitled to respect these officers. Of course, it would not be right to condemn the whole police force for the mistakes of the few, but it is really true that while Indianapolis is a beautiful city, with parks, great buildings, and comprehensive R.R. station, the monumental Capital building, excellent R.R. facilities, and many other commendable things, at the time of this story it had very poor protection for its citizens from vicious attacks of its own police ruffians; and this was greatly to its discredit.

With his mind influenced by all that he had passed through, and by what he had seen of the injustice practiced by officers of the law, he decided in his own mind that he would not pay any more fines, and that he would not go to prison any more, no matter what might come. Unwisely concluding that he had no protection and that he would be justifiable in protecting himself even against the officers of the law, he decided to carry his gun, as had been the custom in Kentucky, and that he would not submit to anyone whether a constable or the president of the United States. His statement was, "I will bother nobody; I will attend to my own business; and if any man tries to take my gun, my only protection, it will be his life or mine."

These Kentucky boys were urged to return to their homes and not try to remain in Indianapolis, for it seemed certain that they would get into serious trouble, but, for the reason that they could make more money there than in Kentucky they refused to go. Then Jesse did not like the idea of running away from danger, even tho he knew it was there, for he was brave enough to risk anything and foolish enough to believe he was right in remaining there instead of leaving the danger zone and going where there would be less danger. So he refused to go, and that was his last fatal mistake.

According to the story of this lamentable clash between Jesse Coe and the officers of Indianapolis, he and his friend George Williams had gone to visit some young women of their acquaintance, and tho they were within their rights and not interfering with anyone, a policeman accosted them and gruffly ordered them to "Move on!" Jesse, smarting under injustices and nursing his old grievances was not disposed to submit to the unwarranted interference of this officer. He turned to one of the boys and said, "I can't see where that officer has any right to give us orders to move on when we are not disturbing anyone; I have tried to get along, but I guess this to be the end of things, for I am determined that if any officer around here shall interfere with any of us I'll burn him up."

Those who knew Jesse Coe would go away and not disturb him when they found him in such a frame of mind, so, tho his friends did not realize how much he meant of what he had said, they were afraid of something very serious, so they made efforts to get him out of the city and avoid what they feared would happen. But, as usual, he refused to go away from danger. He considered that he was free and had a right to live wherever he might desire or decide to live. They feared because they knew him to be absolutely fearless. They had heard him rave and scream, "I was born to die;" and they knew that at that time he had no fear of death; so they were anxious to get him away. The writer who is Jesse Coe's own brother, joined with the others in trying to persuade him, but our efforts were all in vain; and we had to give up trying, though we were certain that something terrible would happen to him, or he would do somebody some serious hurt.

It was about 10 o'clock in the morning when Jesse made the remark about what the consequences would be if any officer should interfere with any of them. The day passed on and it was nine at night, and nothing had happened, so the friends thought everything was all right and the immediate danger had passed. But, unfortunately the officers decided to do just what he had said they had better not do, and he had not forgotten what he had said that morning nor had he changed his mind about it, during the day. But, he was still angry and it was an easy matter for him to get into trouble.

The officers were looking for the other boys, and if Jesse had not been so angry and so hasty, four of them would have lived longer. Now, when the officers arrived and asked for the boys for whom they were looking, Jesse, so they told it, stepped back and ran his hand into his bosom, and an officer approached him and asked him what he had on him. Of course, the officer did not know Jesse and did not know how serious was the situation, perhaps if he had he would have been more cautious and would have made an effort to take him at some more fortunate time; but he did not know, hence the results which this story relates.

Jesse had said that no man should ever take his gun from him, and he was ready to make good his threat, so instead of making reply to the officer, he quickly drew his gun and shot both officers, one in the stomach and one in the groin, and then rushed on away from the scene of the trouble. George Williams was no more than a by-stander, yet, because he was with Jesse, and they found an empty shell in his revolver, they charged him with the crime, as well as Jesse Coe, and made him pay the extreme penalty.

This young man, George Williams knew that he had not hurt anyone, so he did not run away, and they got him within an hour after the shooting of the officers. Any honest investigator would easily have found out that George Williams was not guilty of any crime; that he had no part in the shooting of those officers; and consequently that he should not have been punished. But, as is true in thousands of cases, public sentiment was against him, so they found him guilty and he was hanged at Michigan City, Indiana, for a crime which he did not commit, confirming the saying that "The innocent suffer, and the guilty go oft unwhipped of justice."

After he had shot the two officers Jesse did not do as he had said he would, i.e., that when he did shoot anyone he would shoot everybody in reach until he had been shot down; so, instead of doing that he ran on away, losing his hat or throwing it away that it might not help to identify him. From the scene of the shooting he made his way to the home of one of his friends and asked him to lend him a hat, and when the friend asked him what was the matter, his answer was, "Read the papers in the morning and you will know what has happened." He offered a dollar for the hat, but this friend would not accept, so he took the hat and left the house.

It was said that several people came to the house just as Jesse left it, and that even the officers of the law were close behind him when he entered the house, but he escaped in some mysterious way and none of them saw or recognized him. How he got out of the city of Indianapolis was another mystery which no one ever was able to solve, for, within an hour they had a chain of officers around the whole city; but when the morning came, he was gone.

There were many stories told explaining how Jesse Coe outwitted the officers of Indianapolis and the spies everywhere and got back to Pea Ridge, Kentucky and to the Coe Colony, but that remained a mystery even unto the end. In this case of Jesse Coe, history repeated itself. In early chapters of the Chronicles was told the story how Riley was concealed in his Mother's house, even back in the time of slavery; so it was with Jesse Coe who was concealed for more than two full years, while they were searching for him all over the country, but in vain.

This poor, misguided member of the Colony might have remained in concealment for many years but for the fact that his health began to fail as the result of the long, close confinement, and tired and weary of this forced confinement he came out of hiding and allowed himself to be frequently seen; and that was the beginning of the end for Jesse Coe, as always there have been Judases to betray for a few pieces of silver, or some other form of profit.

In this case, the betrayer was one Claude Andrews who was supposed to be a friend to Jesse and to the Coe Colony, but who proved to be an enemy and a traitor. No doubt if Claude Andrews had known before what he did afterward he would not have lured Jesse Coe away from his friends and protection and killed him for a reward, for Claude Andrews suffered much as the penalty for his treachery, and but for the earnest effort of some who counseled peace, he would have paid with his life, it would have been the old Scripture penalty of "an eye for an eye and a tooth for a tooth." And who can say that such treachery did not deserve all that he did suffer.

When the news reached the Colony that Jesse Coe had been killed, and by a man who had called himself Jesse's friend, the others of the Colony were aroused and again took up their arms. For awhile it looked as if the whole Colony might be wiped out, not because of the attitude of others toward them but their attitude toward others, for they were inclined to pour out their vengeance on all who might cross them. Of course this was wrong, but they were so terribly enraged at the treachery of one who had professed to be a friend and proved to be an enemy, and they began to wonder how many of the professed friends might really be their enemies.

Just at this time the Colony was saved from further bloodshed through the influence of a woman, Cassie Wagner, daughter of Bill Coe, who was very religious and was called "Mother Wagner." "Mother Wagner" came from Indianapolis, professing and preaching sanctification; with the Bible in her hand and a prayer on her lips; and she even claimed to be able to hold communion with the dead. She preached and prayed until she almost lost her voice; and she urged the members to live in peace; not to kill for revenge but to go and leave it all with the Lord who would in His own time set all things right. This preaching and pleading had great effect on the Coe Colony; they became calm; they decided not to take vengeance, as had been decided previously; and as Joan of Arc saved France by leading to war, this woman, this Christian woman; "Mother Wagner" saved the Colony from further blood-shed by leading them into the peace which she was preaching to the world. And right here comes the temptation to enlarge on this thought to the extent of saying, there is in the world no greater influence for good than that of an honest, sincere, conscientious, Christian woman!

Reverting once more to the tragedy which cost the lives of those officers and which was fatal to the happiness and the very life of poor Jesse Coe, the writer of the Chronicles feels inclined to comment on the newspaper publicity, and especially to condemn the attitude of the Negro paper published in Indianapolis, Indiana, which was very unfair and cruel in its attitude and its publication of the account of the tragedy.

The Morning Star, of Indianapolis was quite conservative in its account, publishing the news of the tragedy without trying to explain how it happened or who was in fault, since there were conflicting reports and theories. The Indianapolis News was not so generous and fair as was the Star, but there is the possibility that the publishers of the News thought they were fair, and right. Perhaps too, they acted on the theory that "might makes right," and, because it concerned one of the trampled element, and there was no real danger in assuming such an attitude, they were at liberty to publish what they chose, and could do so without fear of any serious consequences.

Previously this scribe had thought well of the ability and the integrity of George L. Knox, who was the editor and publisher of the Freeman, at the time of this lamentable tragedy, but that opinion was entirely altered after reading the account of this affair in his issue of September 5, 1908, for it was doubtless unfair, and he had gone out of his way to offend and injure those who had never done him injury in any way. Under these circumstances one would be inclined to wonder just what could have been the motive of this man or if by any means he had profited by this unfair and inexcusable thrust at those who had never done him harm.

In Mr. Knox's article was this statement, "It is to be hoped that the Jesse Coe business is a closed incident, for, from beginning to the end it has been a mischief-breeder." Perhaps it is the spirit of this Knox editor which is responsible for much of the confusion in the world today. He did not seek to find out the truth but rushed into print with his unfounded statements. Perhaps such weak-kneed creatures as Mr. Knox are responsible for much of the literal and figurative slavery of all ages. It would be impossible to enslave a man like Jesse Coe for he would be willing to die for his freedom and for what he believed to be right, but a man like this editor would be almost certain to sell himself and his own people as black folk were sold into slavery, in order to get profit for himself.

Now, as to the statement that "from beginning to end it has been a mischief-breeder," one would be inclined to ask, "Is a man a 'mischief-breeder' because he questions the right of another to abuse him without a cause, and to drive him from the side walk or from any other public place, without offering a reason, or when he is interfering with no one and breaking no law?" Again he would be inclined to ask, "Has an officer, just because he is an officer, the right to abuse and attack a citizen, arrest him at will, without a summons, and the individual be forbidden to 'talk back' to him, just because he is an officer. From what he wrote it seems that Mr. Knox was of the opinion that the officer of the law has all of the rights and all the authority, and that the citizen has no right that the officer is bound to respect — and that in this free country where men are conceded to have "inalienable rights!"

Mr. Knox, at the time of these events, lived right there in Indianapolis and doubtless very often visited the "monument square" where high above the ground are bronze figures representing those 'mischief-breeders' who gave their lives that he might enjoy the freedom which he then enjoyed. Chief among the figures of the group is that of one George Clark, who was one of the chief 'mischief-breeders,' and one who played an important part in wrenching the country from the dominance of Great Britain. The trouble started with "mischief-breeders" who resented the abuse of power and the trampling of their rights by the Mother Country, and who rose up and cast off the yoke and made this a free country.

But men of the spirit which Mr. Knox seemed to approve are never known to resist oppression but just to surrender to conditions and make no struggle against them. They suffer themselves to be kicked around and abused in any and every way and enter no protest and make no effort at improvement of conditions. But, as long as men believe in what is represented by the Statue of Liberty at the apex of that Indianapolis monument, they will not just tamely submit to oppression, but will contend, and struggle, and fight — and if need be, will DIE!

This was the spirit of the unfortunate, misguided and persecuted Jesse Coe; it was the spirit of the Coe Colony; it is the spirit of those who still survive, whether living in the cities or in the mountains of Kentucky; and it is the spirit of every man who appreciates liberty, honors the right, and who shares the courage of the founders of the nation, and of those who have, in all of its wars fought for the prosperity and perpetuity of it.

Just when the members of the Colony were beginning to hope anew for peace and relief from the strife of the years, there came another blow, this time involving that stalwart defender of this people, Calvin Coe, the hero of many battles, yet he was not entirely blameless, as the facts will show. The trouble grew out of the fact that Calvin fell in love with a woman whose name was Judy Jane Scott and she agreed to marry him. Because this Miss Scott was a white woman, they were refused license to marry because the state law forbade such intermarriage. Chagrined by the refusal and the disappointment this woman made the proposition that they live together out of wedlock.

Of course Calvin knew this was a violation of the law of God and the law of men; he knew that it would bring criticism and would make trouble, especially because of the prejudice against intermixing of the races; but he did not resist the temptation to assert his rights. Miss Scott said, "I am twenty-five years old, and I ought to be the judge of what is best for me; I am a free woman and do not need anyone to tell me what to do or what is best for me to do; so I shall do as I please." Speaking directly to Calvin, she said, "Now I am willing that we shall live our lives together regardless of the law, no matter what may be the consequences." And Calvin agreed and they began their lives together in defiance of the law and of opinion of their neighbors.

After children began to come into the home, under those circumstances representatives of the law harassed them and gave them much trouble, but they continued to live together and to them were born seven or eight children. Finally they sent Calvin Coe to prison for five years, after his wife had been allowed to die in prison. But, when Calvin came out of jail he did not have the same ideas that his brother John had when he was released from prison. When he reached home he sought for his gun and said, "Well, if it had to be done, I guess I would do it all over again." He added, "From now on I shall not take what I have taken; I will not stand what I have stood; I shall fight my way thru;" and all knew that Calvin was not joking.

Calvin Coe was the one who had fought his own battles and the battles of others; he had been the leader in the protection of the Colony; he had made many sacrifices for his kinfolk. And he considered that he had some rights which should be respected. He gave further expression to his views and decisions in these words: "Men today are selfish; they use all they can and then, they throw away what they cannot use, rather than give such to others who are in need; and even those who pretend to preach the Gospel fail to practice that Gospel which they preach; by their actions they deny that all men should have equal opportunities to make an honest living and the privileges of enjoying what they honestly earn."

His concluding remarks were, "I have always fought for the right; for that reason many people have been against me; enemies have frustrated my plans and spoiled my prospects; but I shall not give up; I shall fight till I die; and if I do not live to see the day when righteousness shall prevail and men shall be judged by character and not by color, race, or nationality, I will have done my part to bring this about; I shall fight for the right, always, even unto the end of my days."

After the killing of Jesse Coe, in 1908, there was left a smoldering fire that had not been extinguished as late as 1920, and the chief actor in the next deplorable drama was Leslie Coe, son of Ora Coe, great grandson of Ezekiel Coe, and commonly known as "Big Less." This young man had begun to practice the evil habits of the older boys, and thereby he came to grief and brought more sorrow on his relatives of the Colony. Like the trouble of Calvin Coe, the Leslie's sorrow was caused by his interest in a woman.

There came to the Colony a young woman of pleasing appearance and attractive personality and Leslie soon began showing attention to her, and some malicious enemies undertook to break up his courtship by threatening him. Leslie contended that as long as a woman was single he had as much right to show her attentions and try to win her as did anyone else. Another young man was impressed with this girl and endeavored to win her attention, but she seemed not to be interested in him and made an excuse every time he tried to associate with her. So, it is supposed that this man and his friends had decided to take revenge on Leslie Coe.

This fellow was not brave enough to come out in the open and fight but hid away and shot from ambush, wounding Leslie in the arm, and this made him more determined to protect himself no matter what the circumstances, and he sent warning to the enemies that he was prepared and would defend his life to the very end. Later, John Coe, (Little John) and Leslie were coming from John's home when someone fired at them. Little John turned and ran in the direction from which the report came, but the assaulters had made a rapid retreat, for having missed their mark they knew it would fatal to remain within reach of the two marksmen.

The wound being only a flesh wound in the arm, Leslie soon recovered, and he was always on the lookout for trouble and ready to take care of himself. After that occurrence, strange things did happen around in the Pea Ridge Settlement. Men would disappear and there would be found no trace of them. Now and then a man would be found dead and no one would know when nor how he died. Enemies on the outside would threaten, worry, tantalize, intimidate, and do everything possible to annoy and discourage the boys of the Colony, hoping, perhaps, to drive them away from their homes.

Bill Sloan, the revenue officer of that district had heard many stories concerning Calvin Coe, and it seemed that he had decided to test the truth of what he had heard. Meeting Calvin, one day, he introduced himself and was greeted by Coe, in return. After the greeting, this officer said to Calvin, "I learn that you are a pretty tough character and I am telling you to prepare yourself to go with me." Speaking for his folk he said, "Why Mr. Sloan, we never defy an officer of the law. You have a perfect right to come after me and I do not blame you for it, if you have something against me, or if I have violated the law."

Surprised and somewhat dazed by the sudden occurrence, Coe remarked, "If I am your prisoner, I suppose I will have to go with you." Then it was that Bill Sloan said, "Well, I haven't got no summons now, but I just want you to know that if I do come after you, you will go with me, and I thought I had just as well tell you now, so that you will understand what to expect when I do come." Calvin's reply was, "Mr. Sloan, I cannot remember that I have done anything contrary to the law, but I was showing respect for you as an officer of the law." The officer's reply was, "Now don't get saucy with an officer." Calvin became very angry, realizing that this man had been threatening him when he had no charge against him and no summons for him, and, as they were riding side by side, he reached over, pushed the officer's hat back and said, "Look here, Bill Sloan, your face looks just like mine to me; I am a man, and you are just a man like me; I tell you now, you never can arrest me and take me anywhere unless I am willing to go with you." He concluded, "Now, since you have talked as you have don't you come around here and try to arrest anybody unless you want to get into serious trouble." Sloan turned and rode away without uttering another word; but he never disturbed Calvin again.

On another occasion, when Calvin Coe was out without his gun he met two young men who thought they could take advantage of his condition. Quickly drawing his gun one of them said, "Now we have you just like we want you and just like we can handle you; we know you are a bad character, so what do you say now?" When he asked, "What is your business here?" The answer was, "To give you a good thrashing." Without speaking another word, Calvin sprang forward, seized the arm of the boasting fellow and took the gun from him. He marched both of them on to his own house, got his gun, and then threw the other gun to the owner and said, "I would not take advantage of you; you have your gun and I have mine; what will you do?" Realizing the danger this intruder begged to be let off promising never to bother him again. Calvin allowed him to go, but warned him that he had better never make such an attempt again.

CHAPTER SIXTEEN
AND THE STORY ENDS

———◆✦◆———

Through all the vicissitudes of the Coe Colony, the "defensive alliance" which they formed remained intact. As has been previously emphasized, they were not aggressive in initiating trouble; they were lovers of peace; the older ones were willing to make many concessions in the interest of peace; and ever the younger ones, with few exceptions, fought always and only on the defensive. If a member got into trouble thru his own wrong-doing, the other would sympathize with him; help him in any way possible; see to it that no advantage was taken of him, and that no mob should take the law into its hands and do violence; but it was their policy not to encourage and sanction any act of imposition of lawlessness even by one of their own. Notwithstanding this, they invariably would protect their own no matter what the cost.

To the south of the Colony lived a family named Webb. This family had trouble with some of their neighbors who had sought to take advantage of them, and they had reported to the "Coe defenders" that they expected these neighbors to seek to do them harm. They were promised protection if these neighbors or anyone else should seek to do them harm and should do so without provocation on the part of the Webbs. Just as they had expected, one night a number of those enemies slipped up to the house and fired on them, seeking to take their lives without giving them any possible opportunity to defend themselves. When this occurred some of the boys ran out and screamed for help, and their cries were so loud that all the people near heard them and knew they were in trouble.

The news of this attack spread rapidly over the Colony and quite soon men were running with their guns in their hands to protect their friends who were thus disturbed. Knowing the nature and the skill of the defenders the enemies fired their shots and withdrew, so that when the Coe fighters got there no one was to be found. In another case, a woman and her daughter who lived east of the Colony had been threatened, and having sought their protection, they had been taken under the wings of the Coe Colony and given the assurance that they would not be imposed upon, and if so the persons who did it would have to answer to the protectors.

On one occasion, while Calvin Coe was serving a term in the county jail at Burkesville, Kentucky, he had trouble with one of the turnkeys who objected to having Calvin playing his banjo so very much, and he had been warned not to play it again. It seems that there were a goodly number of people who would visit the jail just to hear Calvin play, and that this annoyed the turnkey and resulted in the order that Calvin should not play any more. Cal Coe decided that he would obey the orders, so he put his banjo up, as had been required. But, some of the other boys found the banjo and decided to play it, if Calvin would not do so.

Annoyed because he thought this man had defied him as well as disobeyed him, this officer rushed to the top of the stairs with a pistol in his hand and stood there for a little while asking no questions and saying nothing whatever. Then, suddenly he began raising his gun with it pointing toward Calvin Coe. Like a flash Calvin sprang forward and grabbed the turnkey and his gun before he had opportunity to fire it. As they struggled the gun was fired and the bullet grazed Calvin's arm but did very little injury.

Finding himself no match for the prisoner the jailer called for help and his son went running. When Calvin saw him he knew that he had to deal with two instead of one, so he was prepared for the situation. Holding the old man's head locked in his arm he grabbed the young man around the neck and got his neck in the lock of his elbow, he was about to choke both of them to death; but a number of the prisoners begged him not to kill them, and he then got control of himself and released them, after he had threatened to give them each "a wooden overcoat," and they had agreed not to bother him again.

Knowing the reputation of the Coes, the people of Burkesville knew that when they heard that Calvin was shot they would be there; and they were right in their conclusions. Guards had been stationed on the side of the town from which they expected the fighters to come, but suspecting something of this kind the boys went around and entered the town on the other side and soon made their way to the jail. They talked to the jailer, demanded to know what the trouble was, and, trembling with fear he told the truth, confessing that it was all his fault and informing them that he had pledged not to disturb Calvin again. They accepted the statement of the jailer, saw that Calvin was not seriously hurt, and then took their departure. They explained that they were not seeking trouble; did not want to hurt anyone or make any trouble; and that their only object was to protect their own and that they would do so no matter what the cost. The jailer kept his word and Calvin Coe was never again mistreated in any way during his entire time in that prison.

In spite of all that had occurred, all the unfortunate events, all of the tragedies, all of the bloodshed, and of the knowledge of the determination of those people to defend themselves to the uttermost, a big bully named Will Long took chances, interfered and paid for his folly with his life, as he had been told he would do if he persisted in his meddling. But, even in this case those who brought his life to an end were within their rights and were protecting themselves and their own.

A man had been killed. He was killed as the result of meddling with the affairs of other people. He was killed while attempting to kill others. But, he was found dead within the boundaries of the Coe Colony, therefore some of the tribe must pay the penalty. The killing of Will Long could easily have been avoided, for no one bore him any enmity until he initiated the trouble that ended in his death. A man of Long's experience ought to have known that the man who goes into the home of another and acts unbecomingly takes his life in his own hands — and especially when he is dealing with such people as the Coe folk. But he seemed not to realize his danger; so he paid for his folly the dearest possible price.

Will Long had been warned to stay away from the Colony; he had been told what to expect if he persisted in his interference; from what he knew of the Coes he should have understood that what was said was no idle threat; but he ignored all of these and was killed. There never was a clearer case of self-defense, or justifiable homicide, yet the law picked up two young men of the Colony and sent them to the State prison for fifteen years. This was one of the most evident instances of injustice in the history of courts and judges.

The facts were that Leslie Coe had warned this man Long to stay away from the Colony, and when he heard the noise of the shots fired and saw that another effort at assassination had been made, he went running, and as he ran he thought of past events. There came into his mind these facts; his uncle John had been fired on from ambush; the enemies had been annoying them and trying to harm them for many years; and he remembered that he also had been shot from ambush and his arm and been partially paralyzed by the shot. So all these things were running through Leslie's mind as he went running down to where it had been reported that "Will Long was raising hell."

It was reported that there were four of the intruders, but no one knows just how many were there. When Leslie ran up he did not ask any questions; did not seek to find out anything about the identity of the enemies; he knew they were there for trouble and he ran on to defend his own, as all of the tribe was sworn to do, and to do at any cost. As the intruders began to run, Leslie raised his gun and began to fire. The intruders were soon out of sight, except one, Will Long who could not run because one of Leslie's bullets had found its mark and Will Long was dying.

Leslie Coe did not intend that any of those unprincipled fellows should get away, but, after he had fired the first shot he could not shoot another, because they had run so fast and were out of sight. The next morning Will Long was found dead, but no one would confess to knowing anything about how he met his death nor when he was killed. But the officers examined empty shells found near the body and traced those shells to the gun owned by Leslie and John and accepted this as evidence of their connection with the killing; so they were arrested, accused, indicted, tried and convicted and given a sentence of fifteen years. Leslie served about five years of his term and died of scrofula, but before he died he told the truth concerning the killing; that he had killed Will Long, and that his uncle John had nothing to do with it; and on this testimony John was pardoned.

While we must admire and commend the spirit of those two young men who refused to make confessions, because they feared they would not get justice, yet we must condemn the folly of Leslie in allowing his uncle John to make a martyr of himself and serve his prison term, when he was innocent. He feared that they would not get justice, yet he allowed injustice to be done to his kinsman; and John was loyal to the pledge of the Colony and would not tell the truth for fear of hurting Leslie, when the whole truth might have saved them both. While there was danger of injustice, yet it might have been as in the case of Calvin Coe, the judge might have recognized the truth that a man has the right to defend himself and his own, and to kill in the protection of life. But they both did what they thought best, and, after all men are judged by their intentions more than by their deeds.

The majority of the older ones of the Coe Colony had either gone to their rest or had surrendered the reins of government to the younger ones, and these younger ones were of a different type from their ancestors. They lacked the tact, the patience, and the peace-loving spirit of the older ones. In them was more of the tendency to resent and to take revenge. Then there had grown up a spirit of extravagance, so that they seemed inclined to spend what they made on foolish and useless pleasures. And there was not the spirit of industry, as had characterized the older ones of this remarkable Colony; so that some were genuinely alarmed.

Viewing with great concern and genuine alarm the tendencies of the young people of the Colony to drift from the way of safety and to depart from the landmark of their fathers, and impressed with the necessity for doing something to halt this drift and save the people from the inevitable consequences, Thomas E. Coe, who had been principal of the school for fifteen years decided to make such an effort. Having urgently invited all the members of the Colony to attend the closing of his school, Thomas E. took advantage of the occasion to give them the advice contained in this closing narrative. They gathered there, the older ones to show their appreciation of the work being done, and the younger ones, out of curiosity to see what was to be done and to hear what was to be said.

The first statement was, "Friends of the illustrious Colony, we are here as the descendants of some of the best people that ever walked on God's green earth; we have in us the stock of which we may well be proud. The young people here are descendants of people who were true, loyal and sincere in their relations to one another and to the world. Nearly all of the older people have gone to their rest and to their eternal reward, and we who constitute the younger generation are to continue the work they began."

Seeing that he had their attention to an unusual degree, the speaker proceeded to deliver the address which he prepared, as follows:

"Our parents and grandparents were God-fearing, peace-loving people. They desired to live in peace with all mankind. While the history of the Colony is one of strife and blood-shed, these unfortunate things were forced upon them. They were not the ones who began the trouble, for they were willing to let others live and prosper as they expected others would do for them. They were brave, they were valiant in self-defense; they did not hesitate to risk their lives, even to give their lives in the defense of one another, or in the support of principles which they believe to be right. These ancestors of ours were honest and honorable, choosing rather to suffer injustice than to do others wrong. And the record of their lives, as a whole, will give evidence of the truth of these statements.

"Now, young people, you who are descendants of these noble and honorable people, they have gone to their reward and their work is left for you to do. They have bequeathed to you one of the richest of legacies. Not so much of gold and silver, houses and broad acres, but they have left you the heritage of bravery, honor, honesty, justice, courage, and genuine nobility of character as it has been the lot of few to receive. But the question is, 'What will you do with your rich heritage?' Will you prize it and improve on it, or will you foolishly waste it and lose it?

"Both God and man will hold you responsible, and the more of light, of intelligence you have, the more responsible you will be, and the more both God and man will require of you; and this is in keeping with both justice and reason.

"You know nothing of slavery and its oppression; you know little of the struggles and sufferings of the early days of our freedom and of the Colony. What you have heard doubtless seems to you like a dream or an interesting story well told. You know in some measure the hatred and the prejudice with which the older people had to contend, but, even then, you cannot understand what material they were forced to put into this superstructure of worthiness and usefulness which it was their privilege and their joy to build.

"I want to appeal to the young women and urge them to do all that they can to uphold the spirit of the fathers. I would urge them to help the men to stand up and be men, and by no means help to drag them down. The greatest influence in any man's life is a good woman; and the most harmful influence is that of an evil woman. If you encourage the young men to go down, by the very nature of your associations with them they will pull you down to their level; so I urge you to be strong, to remain living on the higher plane, and then to do all that you can to help the young men to stand up and be men worth the name, man!

"As I look into your faces I see all colors, white, and red, and black, showing the divisions of colors and races, but in spirit, in interest, in loyalty to one another, in striving to do the right and keep to the mark set by the fathers, there should be no division among us. The colors of our skins are matters of circumstances and environments, but these have nothing to do with our character, our honor, our honesty, our industry; in these we should be united, for they constitute character — and life, itself.

"In one way we should be what might appear to be selfish. We should be loyal and true to members of the Colony, sharing our possessions, extending sympathy, comforting in distress and protecting in time of peril, as did our forefathers. On the other hand we should deal honestly and generously with our neighbors, remembering that no person is independent and there is no one but needs the friendship and good-will of others. Therefore, as member of the community we cannot afford to be selfish and clannish to the extent of forgetting the interests and necessities of our neighbors.

"Again I would call your attention to the subject of peace; for tho they were misunderstood, our ancestors loved peace; and they hated strife, confusion and blood-shed. It may be observed that many of the young people of the Colony, especially the young men, are disposed to trample on the rights of others, and I would urge them to be honest and fair in this respect. Some are inclined to be indolent, but without industry no one can make an honest living and live a happy life. Revenge is another spirit to be discouraged, for vengeance is not right, and it usually ends in trouble for those who seek revenge.

"Summing up: Do right; live in peace; work for an honest living; show kindness, meet the friendly spirit of your neighbor with a like spirit; be industrious and do not waste your living; take your part and defend yourselves when necessary but do not impose on others and cause trouble; go to school, study, and improve your minds, so that you will be able to discharge your duties as citizens of this country; in your lives, honor God, the God of the universe, and by right living honor your forefathers who have gone to their reward and left you to build on the foundation they laid."

In this closing address, Thomas E. Coe, summed up what was the spirit and what were the sentiments of the founders of the illustrious Coe Colony of Pea Ridge District, and the rules by which they endeavored to live. Of course there were exceptions. There were a few wild, unscrupulous fellows who were discreditable to the Colony and whose actions were severely condemned by them, but, as a whole the disposition was and the efforts were toward community peace and harmony. Also, in this address, the world may read the sentiments of those of the Colony who still survive, for still the strongest desire of the remnant is for peace, friendship and goodwill toward all men.

Now, I am inclined to turn once more to the Bible for language with which to close this narrative; therefore, paraphrasing, I write, "But, all the deeds of the stalwart, brave, courageous, good-natured, God-fearing and peace-loving, are they not written on the minds and in the characters of men? And who can tell how much has been written on the records eternal, of the deeds of those who, in their own way, according to their opportunities made their humble but inestimable contribution to betterment of humanity and to the advancement of this nation." Who can tell?

ADDENDA
I
RUMINATIONS OF SAMUEL COE
PRESENTING CREDENTIALS

These facts may read like fiction, but they are facts, nevertheless, and there are living witnesses which might be secured if necessity should require, even tho we are this distance from the days of the actual occurrences related. The writer considers himself qualified to tell this story; to do justice to all concerned; and he bases his claims for fitness on his access to knowledge — accurate knowledge concerning the actors in the drama, and the results of their actions.

First, while he did not live "on the other side of the flood," the slavery period, he did live through the period immediately following slavery. He heard from the actors and from witnesses the stories of the slave period; he listened to the relation of these stirring scenes and they are so firmly fixed in his memory that to him they seem like living, personal experiences. So vivid were the impressions of these that he scarcely can differentiate between what he heard and what he saw.

Second, the writer, in fact is one of the immediate descendants of those who came out of slavery; he was associated with those of this class of stalwart heroes who came out of the darkness of bondage into the glorious light of liberty. Tho young, he was familiar with the eventualities of the unrighteous struggle to prevent the progress of his people and others of the same group; and these he could not forget. He witnessed the fierce and tragic struggle between the aspiring people of his own tribesmen and their contemporaries, under their efforts toward peace and the cruel injustices done them; and his youthful mind was impressed with the fortitude with which they endured these injustices.

Third, it was his privilege to grow up among the first of the "younger generation," witness the effect and influence of both heredity, and environment, as these were manifest in the lives, temperaments and the very warp and woof of their character. He was privileged to study effects of association; parental laxity and evil example; and of ignorance, on the part of his own people. He observed, also, the growth and development of that unreasonable, inequitable, accursed thing known as racial prejudice. He had, as thousands of his class, and of their successors, to light against the inclination toward resentment, hatred, and vengeance, in his own heart.

Looking back on the experiences which have been related, this scion of those people and product of those conditions can see the mistakes made by those who were leaders in those days. There are some things of which he could not approve. He realizes that in many instances a little more patience and a little more tolerance might have obviated some of the clashes. He knows that in some instances bloodshed would have been avoided if his own relatives had been a little more conservative. But, taking into consideration all phases of the matter, he unhesitatingly exults in the fact that he has flowing in his own veins the blood of these intrepid heroes of whom he is writing in

"Chronicles of the Coe Colony."

The scribe too, has lived thru the period extending from those daring, dangerous, heroic, tragic days of this period of national and racial development. He lived in the section in which slavery was in force and in which it was followed by an era of strife and destruction which language never can accurately describe. For a number of years he has lived in sections where slavery did not exist, and especially in "bleeding Kansas", where human rights and human degradation met in mortal combat, which struggle had its effect in hastening the Civil War and the liberation of those who were held in cruel bondage.

Having lived among those and still living among these conditions; suffering restrictions and discriminations and yet enjoying a large measure of freedom; seeing the evils of this age, noting bribery and graft, corruption and injustice, malfeasance in office; conscious of the injustices and inequities of our judiciary and the inexcusable blunders in the administration of our penal system, the writer judges himself in a small measure capable of rendering judgment in regard to these things. At least he feels justifiable in expressing his views in reference to them.

Now, for what they are worth, whether they shall be accepted or rejected, whether they shall bring him applause or condemnation, whether he shall be considered a conservative or a deluded fanatic, in these ruminations he is expressing his honest convictions of these problems, these modern-day problems as honestly and as conscientiously as he has told the story of the other period. So, the ruminations follow.

II
PROHIBITION

Previously I have told of the death of Joseph Coe, in a hospital in Indianapolis, from alcoholic poison, but here I would affirm that Joseph Coe was only one of many thousands who have died from the same cause, since the passage of the Eighteenth Amendment to the Constitution of the Untied States. As I puzzle my brain in regard to this law, I am inclined to wonder if I am mentally unbalanced or the other people of the United States. I am convinced that the majority of the people of this nation would rather be right than wrong, but their ideas and the attitude on this drink question, surprise and puzzle me; and, I am convinced that if they continue as they are going they will wreck this nation.

Having lived in Kansas City, Kansas for twenty-five years, I have had opportunity to see what prohibition will do for a city in an economic way. Here is a summary of what it has done here: In 1910 a prohibition officer named Trickett caused the padlock law to be applied to one hundred places where they sold booze, and nearly all of these places have been vacant since, quite a number of these houses were torn down and the lots still are vacant. Much property has changed hands because of heavy taxes; streets have gone unpaved because of lack of funds; and many are the other items of economic loss, following the enforcement of this Amendment.

Turning to the Bible, the good Book on which we base our hopes, we read in St. Mark, the 10th chapter and the 18th verse, "They shall take up serpents, and if they drink any deadly thing it shall not hurt them." I have been inclined to think that perhaps the law-makers of the country passed the 18th Amendment to the Constitution in order to kill off all the bad people, for, if you are good, you can drink anything and it will not hurt you. Another thing, it is difficult to understand some of these people who profess to be Christians. We find in Mark 7:16, "There is nothing from without a man that entering into him can defile him;" and yet the Christian people have raised war over drink and caused many people to be put to death. When Judas had betrayed the Son of Man, and the officers had come to take Him, we read in St. John 18:10-11, where it is said, "Then Simon Peter having a sword, drew it and smote the high priest's sergeant, and cut off his right ear.": Then said Jesus unto Peter, "Put up thy sword into the sheath; the cup that my Father hath given me shall I not drink it."

This passage is cited to show that the Lord does not intend that one should not try to save another; and I believe if the Lord were here, in the flesh, He would tell those who are trying to establish prohibition, "Put up thy sword; we are not here to destroy men's lives, but to save them." The homes that have been torn up and the death and destruction caused by the efforts to enforce prohibition would cause one to stop and wonder who shall be responsible for all these, in the judgment day.

I am thinking of the war period of our country, when the munition plants were running night and day, and in shifts, and of the period just following the close of the war when these many thousands of workers had to find other places to sell their labor — I refer to the three millions of unemployed men turned out of the army, with nothing to do. Then they stopped the sale of whiskey and sent many others out of employment.

At this time, the country was in a deplorable condition; the farmer could find no market for his product; many of them left their farms and went elsewhere; and all of this was because of the folly of the law-makers who had cut off his best customer. He has his apples, peaches, barley, rye and potatoes all of which he had been using to make alcohol, and found them useless on his hands, because of this law. Thus it is evident that the law played havoc with the interests of the farmer and other working men.

Not long ago two great conventions met to nominate a man for President of the United States. The Republicans met in Kansas City, Mo., and the Democrats in Houston, Texas. It was necessary that each party should write a new platform. Amusing it was to listen to the speeches at both conventions, tell what they intended to do for the farmer, when anybody with common sense knows that when you stop using anything there is no market for it, and time and labor putting it on the market must be lost.

It was ridiculous to hear these law-makers making speeches when they had voted to take from the farmer the best market that he had. Perchance, I heard the great evangelist Billy Sunday upbraiding the saloon men and saying they should go into some other business, and sitting there, I wondered, "Now what sort of business was left for these people to go into?" In my mind I saw the farmer struggling to find a better market for his produce; the baker trying to sell more bread; servants sitting in clothing stores waiting for someone to come in and buy; the coal-miner was compelled to stop his production for a year because the market was flooded.

To continue the enumeration of particulars, the foundries shut down because they had no market for their output; hat-makers, shirt-makers and dress-makers must change their styles before they could continue to sell; and many other kinds of businesses were looking for a better market for their goods. When I noted all of these things I could not understand what Billy Sunday or any other well-informed man could have on his mind. How could their ideas be put into effect if they shut down the 'breweries' and the distilleries and filled the country with unemployed.

Another strange thing about the law-makers. It seemed to be very easy to raise several billions of dollars during the war, but when it came to appropriating money enough to curb the Mississippi River, they could hardly find money enough to just clean the channel. After voting to shut down the greatest industry of the country, they preferred to give back the tax money to millionaires than to improve the country by putting the surplus labor to work.

It has always been a matter of surprise, to me, that the lawmaking bodies did not take more interest in labor than they have, heretofore. But for the fact that the laboring classes form their labor-unions and thereby protect themselves and that others form unions for their own protection, much greater would be the suffering. It seems that unless you are needed as a soldier, you can go and jump into the river, as far as the government is concerned.

At this time, considering these things, my mind reverts to the case of Joseph Coe and his application to Bedford for bread, with the results that followed. It is reported that Booker T. Washington said, "You can't make a Christian out of a hungry man;" and everybody with good sense knows that it is true. All who believe that it is possible to turn loose twenty millions of men in this country, with nothing to do by which to make a living and then prevent bootlegging, rum-running, house-prowling, stealing, robbing, and murder is indeed non compositeness. Only a buffoon could be persuaded to believe that there could be peace, contentment and law and order under such conditions.

If you should go thru Pea Ridge, Kentucky, and if you should be fortunate enough to get a drink, you would not get something that would take your life in twenty-four hours, or eat out the lining of your stomach and soon take you out of the world. True some of these people are greedy; they want to make money, but they would not make and sell just anything for sake of money. But, in almost every city of this country there are people who make and sell poison, in the form of drink, caring nothing for the lives of the people, just so they are making money easy.

Many people are worrying about those who drink; it is serious when people overdo, in this matter; but the facts are that among the better element of people you can find more that drink than that do not drink. It is my opinion that you are more apt to get a favor from the man who is fair to himself than from the one who is not, for you cannot expect a man who will not be fair to himself to ever be fair dealing with anybody else. As for me, I reason that if I deny myself anything in this world that has been placed here by the forces of nature for my benefit is my own fault.

In my experience, I lay claim to the fact that at one time, whiskey saved my life. Of course, I might have lived on without the whiskey, but I am candid in my belief that my life is due to this use of the stimulant. But, perhaps, some who read the story, and especially these ruminations will decide that it would be better that I should have died. Well, they think I am wrong, and I think they are wrong, and that is the cause of the strife and bloodshed thru all the ages. However, in my views on the mooted question of prohibition, I am far from being alone, for many of the best people in the world share my views, or I share their views, in thinking and contending that a man has the right to think for himself and to choose for himself.

If you would discuss prohibition with the people of the Pea Ridge section they would call your attention to the economic side of it. They will tell you that their land does not bring so much and they must make the best of what it does bring. They will explain that a bushel of corn that will sell for a dollar in its natural state will not pay; that they can take that same bushel of corn, make it into alcohol, or whiskey, making from three to four gallons out of a bushel, and that it will bring from eight to ten dollars a gallon.

They would admit that making whiskey is against the law, and they will argue that the men who made this law have not devised any way for them to make their living. They have said what a man shall not do, but they have given him no specific way by which he can use his grain and get as much out of it as in the other way. Of course, we have agreed to let the majority rule in this country, but we have not the proof that the majority of the people in this country favor prohibition, and this is another case of unfairness and of taking advantage of people and their circumstances.

All who are in their right minds know that prohibition is wrong, and I doubt if anyone can tell just how the country drifted into this condition. When we go back to the first country that adopted prohibition we realize that it has almost perished from the map of the world. The Arabs were once a great people, and I will not say that prohibition is responsible for their decay and their fall, but when I look about Kansas City and see the destruction wrought by prohibition I conclude that perhaps it is true that it is responsible for the downfall of the Arabs.

All who are familiar with history know that England had prohibition at one time. They called it "the blue law", and I consider it well named, for whatever stops the consumer stops the wheels of industry; and it did not take the English folk long to find that out, and that is the reason why "Pussy-foot Johnson" could not get very far over there, with his prohibition program. The Czar of Russia stopped the sale of vodka in a night, and while I do not say that caused its downfall, but when I see twenty millions of men in this country, doing everything they can to defy and break the law I realize that we are drifting toward the fate of Russia. And it is to be hoped that the people of this nation will come to their senses before prohibition shall destroy this country.

III
TRUTH-SPIRIT-LOVE
1

The "question of the ages" is the question which Pilate asked the Master, "What is the truth;" the most persistent search thru all the ages has been the search for truth; truth is everywhere, yet who can put his finger on it and say, "There it is." In regards to truth few persons agree. No matter how much you might set forth, someone would doubt it and someone would dispute it, and he would do this in order to appear great in the eyes of the world; yet in John 8:32 we read where Jesus said, "And ye shall know the truth and the truth shall make you free."

The fact is that there are few people who want the truth; few are seeking the truth; most of them are depending on some other fellow to tell them about it; but, if they are not careful it will be as the Lord said in Matt. 15:13-14, "Every plant which my heavenly father hath not planted shall be rooted up;" then "Let them alone; they shall be blind leaders of the blind." When Pilate asked that question about truth, Jesus did not condescend to answer him, for he knew that Pilate was not a searcher after this principle called truth, and He would not indulge his vanity by making reply to his question.

Notwithstanding His refusal to answer Pilate, Jesus in many ways and on many occasions exalted truth and made explanations concerning it. Here are some of the expressions: "Thy Word is truth;" "The truth shall make you free;" "I am the Truth!" Because of our human weaknesses and limitations, God does not attempt to reveal all His truth to us, yet there is much that we might know, if we would seek the truth. Because we do not know we are constantly enslaving our minds and tugging at that which is immovable, when if we knew the truth we would be free from such conditions — we would have a better understanding of the things of the world and of the possibilities of mankind. Knowing the truth one can map out his own plan of conduct, according to the general requirements of righteousness, and justice, and fairness, without being so much dependent on others for his guidance.

The wise King Solomon asked the question, "What is love?" And I would change it to the extent of asking, "What is life?" We live in the world where the God whom we profess to serve permits even small, creeping things to live, yet, in many cases, it seems that we want to take God's business in hand and run it for Him, and to destroy whatever we will and preserve whatever we will. When we are inclined to act in this way we would do well to remember the fate of those who attempted to build the tower of Babel, a tower that would reach to God's throne. God looked down upon them, and to Him, their tower was no more than an ant-hill, or a hole made by a little bug, as his winter home.

Because the Great God knows our weaknesses and because He is merciful, He warns us of danger and teaches us how to live out our days in peace, and if we do not obey him, and our days are shortened, we cannot hold Him responsible. It is like a child who is warned by its parents not to go near the fire. If the child disobeys his parents and gets burned, it is not the parent's fault and they are not responsible. So it is with God in dealing with us. This we call free moral agency.

This God is Lord of the universe; He is all Spirit; and He is also Love, and TRUTH; and tho He is merciful He cannot lay hold upon us, restrain us and keep us from danger, because He has made us free. The thing for us to do is to ally ourselves with the truth He taught, seek information from His Word, follow His commandments rather than seek information from men who are themselves limited in wisdom.

In this day it is certain that most people are interested in themselves, in getting what they desire and advancing their interests rather than in seeking after truth. They are not trying to get a better understanding of their fellowmen. They are satisfied with what knowledge they have and are not seeking for the truth. Since we come into the world without knowledge, and must gain knowledge from contact with others, it behooves us to gather in knowledge from every possible source. If life depends on knowledge and knowledge is just another term for truth, we should keep busy seeking the truth wherever it may be possible to find it, in order to be free and to live out our lives in peace.

We find these things and are infinitely more involved in the discussion of truth, yet, tho in all ages there have been some who sought the truth, it has always been and is today, that the great masses are rushing on, hither and thither, some too indolent to seek the truth, and others satisfied with their present condition. These are they of whom the Master was speaking when He said "They close their eyes against the light and their ears against the truth."

2
SPIRIT

The things of the Spirit are wonderful, mysterious, baffling, confusing, and who can understand them? There are thousands who have sought the light because they desired to know and to do that which was right. But much of our lack of knowledge is because of our failure to seek the truth and our unwillingness to recognize and honor the truth when found. In my mind it seems reasonable to conclude that the God of all wisdom would reveal more and more of His wisdom if they only would see the light.

Turning to Matthew 7, and beginning at the sixth verse, we read, "Give not that which is holy to the dogs, neither cast ye your pearls before swine, lest they trample them under their feet, and turn again and rend you." Again we read, "Ask, and it shall be given; seek, and ye shall find; knock, and it shall be opened unto you." Then follows, "For every one that asketh, receiveth, he that seeketh, findith, and to him that knocketh it shall be opened." So it is reasonable to believe that any man who seeketh light and truth thru the Spirit shall most surely find that for which he seeks.

Now, the Spirit world is greater than the world of the flesh, for, without spirit all flesh would perish. I shall use a parable: When a house is built the house may be removed, but the earth will remain; in like manner, the flesh which clothes the Spirit may be removed but the spirit remains. We cannot see the spirit; we can never understand its operations; but we can and do witness the operations and influences of it. The mysterious workings of the Spirit were emphasized by the Master when he said to Nicodemus, "The wind bloweth where it listeth and thou hearest the sound thereof but canst not tell whence it cometh or whither it goeth; so is every one that is born of the Spirit."

From the operations of matter we might reason that there are many spirits. This we cannot prove, but we do know there are many operations and spiritual influences; and we do know that somehow there is the spirit of good and the spirit of evil. One of the evidences of the presence and operation of the spirit of evil is the tendency to excuse our own misdeeds and fix the blame on others for their shortcoming. We are inclined to see the evil in others, condemn that evil, while we shut our eyes to our own faults, and judge with tolerance, even when we do recognize and confess our own faults.

Under the influence of the Good Spirit, we would understand that we are in the world in the midst of evil; that we did not create the evil, but are influenced by the spirit of evil and can have no power over the unclean spirits unless it be given us by the God of the Universe. If we will accept the guidance of the Spirit and try to follow that guidance, we will then be slow to condemn others, and we would try to lead others in the right way that they might have peace and their lives might be useful to themselves and to others. In all things we should remember that we are flesh, and that, as Jesus said, God is a spirit and those that worship Him must believe in spirit and in truth.

3
FAITH

In all the ages of the world, from the time that Abraham was called to leave his home and his men and go into a strange land, faith has weighed heavily in the relationship between God and man and in man's adjustment to the will and purpose of God, in human life. It was thru the faith and obedience of Noah, who built the mighty ark, that the world was saved from the universal flood. But, it was the God of heaven that sent Noah into the world that God might have even a few who would serve him and replenish the earth, after the mighty flood.

Again God found it necessary to find a man whom He might trust to lead the world in the path of righteousness and set an example of exalted faith. According to the record of Moses, God found such a man in the person Abram, afterwards called Abraham, and who has been called, "The father of the faithful." In all of God's dealings with men and men's dealings with God, faith has played an important role — and what the world is yet to be, in every sense of the word will depend on faith.

Now, this man Abraham was a Babylonian, living in the days of King Nimrod, and at a time when the people knew very little about the God who is a spirit, so it is a marvel that Abraham should have been willing to trust One whom he had never seen and of whom so little could be known but, that is the very essence of faith. But the God of the universe revealed to Abraham that there was something else to worship beside sun, moon, and stars, fire, wind and water; and this man began his search for the true God — the spiritual God that was invisible and dwelt not in temples made with hands. Searching for God, by faith he found TRUTH, and SPIRIT; and he found joy and profit in worshipping Him.

God Knew the heart of Abraham, but He decided to apply to

him the supreme test, therefore he required of him to offer as a sacrifice his own son, Isaac. God found him a man who was willing to obey His word; willing to endure any test; and as a reward not only did God bless him and bless all the earth thru him, but he was honored in that the Savior of mankind was "of the seed of Abraham." This honor and this distinction came as a reward for his nonquestioning faith in the God who is a Spirit.

John had reference to the faith of Abraham, and the generations who would emulate him in the matter of faith, and when he said, "God is able out of these stones to raise up children unto Abraham."

In this day there is fierce discussion in regard to the birth of Jesus, but that should not worry us. We are in the world; we have father and mother; how we came is a mooted question; but we have the story of Moses in regard to the creation of man, male and female, and of the creation of all things out of nothing, and if we are to live in peace and serve God we must accept the Savior's nativity, by faith, as we do accept by faith these other things which we cannot understand. If we discern God and worship Him at all, it must be by faith for we read, "No man hath seen God at anytime;" and Job's question, "Can a man by searching find out God?"

For further evidence of faith and its benefits, we will consider the life and services of Moses, the leader of the people of Israel in their journey from Egypt to Canaan. We will follow him up into the mountain and watch him as he receives the tablet of stone with Commandments written on them. It was the unswerving faith of Moses which sustained him as he climbed the mountain, to stand in the presence of Jehovah, not knowing what the consequences would be. And it was this faith that sustained him during the trials caused by the doubts and fears and the general waywardness of the people whom he was leading.

We read in Exodus 25:10, "And they shall make an ark of shittim wood; two cubits and a half shall be the length thereof and a cubit and half the breadth thereof, and a cubit and a half the height thereof." Then, in sixteenth verse, "And they shall put into the ark the testimony which I shall give thee." In Deuteronomy we read, 10th chapter two to five, "Take this book of the law and put it in the of the ark of the Covenant of the Lord, your God, that it may be there as a witness against thee." There follows this command, in Numbers 10:33, "And they departed from the mount of the Lord three days journey, and the Ark of the Covenant of the Lord was before them in three days journey, to search for a resting place for them."

The record in Deuteronomy 1:35 reads, "Who went in the way before you, to search you out a place to pitch your tents in, in fire by night to you by what way you should go, and in the day a cloud." In tracing the Ark of the Covenant of the Lord, we read the whole of the sixth and seventh chapters of Joshua. We find in the eighteenth chapter and the first verse, "And the whole congregation of the children of Israel assembled together at Shiloh, and up the tabernacle of the congregation there, and the land was subdued." We find further explanation in I Sam. 4:4, "So the people sent to Shiloh that they might bring from thence the Ark of the Covenant of the Lord of hosts which dwelleth between the Cherabim; and the two sons of Eli, Hophni and Phinehas were there with the Ark of the Covenant of God."

Continuing this discussion read second Samuel fifth chapter, "And the Philistines took the Ark of God and brought it from Ebenezer unto Ashdod." We find also in sixth chapter of Second Samuel, "And the Ark of the Lord was in the country of the Philistines seven months." Turning to the 18th verse this reads, "And take the Ark of the Lord and lay it upon the cart; and put the jewels of gold which you returned him for a trespass-offering, in a coffer by the side thereof, and send it sway, that it may go." And then we find in I Samuel, 7th chapter and first verse, "And men of Kirjath-Jearim came and fetched up the Ark of the Lord, and brought it unto the house of Abinadab, in the hill, and sanctified Eleazar, his son, to keep the Ark of the Lord."

In the second chapter of this book is recorded, "And it came to pass while the Ark abode in Kirjath-Jearim, that the time was long, for it was twenty years." Then follows, II Sam. 6th chapter, but especial attention is called to the 12th verse which reads as follows: "And it was told the King David, saying, "The Lord hath blessed the house of Obededom, and all that pertained unto him, because of the Ark of the Lord.'" So David went and brought the Ark of the Lord from the house of Obededom into the city of David, with gladness. Now, let us refer to I Kings, 8th chapter and first verse, and read, "Then Solomon assembled the elders of Israel, and all the heads of the tribes, the chief of the fathers of the children of Israel unto King Solomon in Jerusalem, that they might bring up the Ark of the Covenant of the Lord out of the City of David, which is Mount Zion." Still tracing the Ark of the Covenant, we lose trace of it, after following from Exodus 25th chapter to Solomon's Temple.

But now, we come to the light again when we read Hebrews 9: 14, "How much more shall the blood of Christ, who thru the eternal Spirit offered Himself without spot, to God, purge your consciences from the dead works to serve the living God?" Here in this history of the journeying of the Ark of the Lord are to found two significant principles. There it represented the invisible God, Creator and observer of all things. Then, the paramount human element was the faith of the people who thru their long period worshipped this unseen God who was invisible, and this by means of the most marvelous faith known to mankind.

It might be added that faith is one of the elements lacking among men today. The great standing armies, expansive navies and other preparations for war are the results of lack of faith of our nation in the integrity and the word of other nations and we never will have peace in the world until faith has been cultivated and restored to its rightful place. When nations will believe the world of other nations and the genuineness of the friendship professed by other nations, then we will see the end of war, and the end of armaments.

4
LOVE

There is no fallacy in the contention that love is an element of Divinity, a part of the God of the universe, for we have the authority of John, the apostle, who uttered that comforting and enlightening truth, "God is Love." Webster defines love, the verb, "to regard with affection;" and as a noun, "Goodwill, fondness, the ones beloved, courtship." There are many other definitions which bring out the various phases of love. However while there are these many definitions, many theories, many variations, and thousands of books have been written on the subject of love, it is doubtful if any one fully understands this subtle principle of such immense importance.

According to many writers love prompts sufferings and sacrifices; it delights in suffering for the one loved; it makes one blind to the faults of the one he loves; and while it is difficult to fathom, as is true of other subtle elements, truth, spirit, faith, it is as real as they. Tho, as is true of other things, you cannot see it, you cannot touch it, you cannot grasp it by means of sense perception; yet it is the most dynamic force in all of the universe; and its ties are the strongest and the most enduring known to mankind.

The highest tribute paid to love and the chiefest explanation of God's attitude toward men will be found in what is termed the "sweetest verse of the Bible," John 3:6, "For God so loved the world that He gave His only begotten Son, that whosoever believeth in him shall not perish but have everlasting life." And Jesus Himself emphasized this towering attitude of love when He declared, "And greater love hath no man than this, that a man would lay down his life for his friend." Jesus invites us, "Come unto me all ye who are burdened and heavy laden, and I will give you rest;" and this is the call of love and the pledge of comfort, and help in distress.

The world needs more of love, and more love for God will mean more love from man to man; and love, operating under such circumstances will solve all the problems of the world. Jesus said, "Thou shalt love they neighbor as thyself," and when one thus loves his neighbor he will not harm him; will not take advantage of his weakness, his ignorance nor his adverse circumstances. Then, the "strong" will bear the infirmities of the weak, and justice and equity will prevail throughout the great world of mankind.

Love often is misunderstood, misrepresented, and no doubt often abused; but love is of God and cannot be a sin. Sex love is no sin; it is God's plan for keeping the world alive. The love of a woman for a man is in keeping with God's plan. But there are other things which parade in the guise of love and it is they that make the trouble. Love, to answer the purpose of God and to benefit rather than hinder mankind means more that the satisfaction of physical, carnal desire. This misconception of love has been the curse of the ages and the cause of many tragedies.

According to the plans of God, holy matrimony between male and female is intended to be a perfect union; the relationship should be spiritual as well as physical; both are intended and both are important. Both beautiful and wonderful is the plan that after communion of the spiritual and the physical we have an illustration of the "incarnation" of love, in a little child, the product of the spiritual and physical union of the two who love each other and are united for that reason.

But any love that ignores the spiritual and fails to ally itself with the Divine, and proves to be but the expression and the satisfaction of the physical is doomed to utter failure! One of the causes of failure in marriage relations is the disposition of many to decide the question of love and marriage for others when they have not been able to make perfect and permanent their own marriage union. But God has not committed this all-important matter to others, tho they may be parents. He has committed it to those who must bear the humiliations, the sufferings and the losses, if they blunder in this respect. While young people should respect the opinions, advice and admonitions of their parents, if they are to be happy, the young people must make their own selections as did their parents.

I am speaking in parables, as the Savior often spoke in parables, and of course there will be those who will not understand, as there were those who did not understand Him. Some fail of understanding because they are naturally dull; but others fail because they want to have their own way. Jesus hinted at this condition when He said, "If I tell you of earthly things, and you do not believe, how much more so if I tell you of heavenly things." And it is true, today, people shut out the truth and go on believing what they desire to believe. Now, whatever may be thought or said, serious is this question of matrimony, for we read, "For this cause shall a man leave father and mother and cleave to his wife; and the twain shall be one flesh."

SUMMARY

On the preceding pages have been set forth the importance, the value, the functions and influences of Truth, Spirit, Faith, and Love. Abraham and Moses are types of faith and Jesus Himself the example and illustration of both Truth and Love, and of the incarnation of spirit in its work of elevating the flesh and binding it to Divinity, thru the Spirit; and all of this it would be well that the world should believe. Believing this, men would have both guidance and inspiration in their efforts to do their best.

No man can be the measure of his own righteousness nor the law of his own conduct; he must know the Truth, be inspired by the spirit, exercise faith in God, in himself and in humanity; and he must have love for God and for mankind. When such shall obtain we shall have the beginning of heaven on earth. Thus inspired and actuated a man would not take advantage of his fellow-man; he would "eat bread with the singleness of heart;" there would be no class distinctions, for it would be recognized that all belong to God.

Under the conditions and circumstances we are discussing men would realize that God is God of all; note that He always sends the sunshine on all and the "rain on the unjust as well as the just;" that He is merciful and sends his blessings upon the good and the evil; and, recognizing man as the masterpiece of the creation of God, every man would deal honestly and righteously with every other man, There would be no more wars; men would not use all kinds of inventions to kill one another and to destroy property; and thus would individuals and nations live together in peace and harmony.

IV
1
PARTY OR POLICY

In attempting to discuss politics it is recognized and conceded that it is a subject understood by very few, if any. In politics, as a system, there is very little of fairness or justice, for the thing uppermost in the minds of those who are seeking office is to best their antagonists, no matter how this is done. It seems to be conceded that a man has the right to say all kinds of unclean things concerning his opponent, in order to win office — but this is far from truth, and love.

There are two principles that ought to obtain — justice and truth, but these are seldom considered in political contests. There are two major parties in this country, the Republican Party and the Democrat Party, but it is contended that the "Croutau" has no party. It is generally accepted that the colored people of this country should support the Republican Party. The contention is that we owe something to it, but this writer contends that such a claim is false. They do not owe anything to the nation, but the nation will be in debt to them for the next hundred years.

They tell us that the Civil War was between the two parties, but the truth is that the war was between the North and the South, rather than between these two parties, and when the subject is properly considered these facts are easily evident; so it is wrong to keep circulating a false report concerning this matter. The truth, the whole truth ought to be told.

In the last national campaign I followed my conviction and supported Al Smith, not because he was a democrat, nor because he was a member of a prominent church, nor because he had been governor of the great State of New York. I supported him because, in my estimation he had been honest with himself and was willing to face the truth in trying to save his country and so I concede to every man the right to vote for whatever candidate he may choose, if in his heart he believes he is the right man for the office.

In the exercise of the rights of franchise we should be very careful and select men because we have faith in their integrity, their honesty and their fairness, not because we like the men nor because they are our personal friends. And, of course there should be no question of selling our vote for it is a sacred thing. In this respect, this truth obtains; if we select men who are square and will deal fairly with all the people, we are apt to have peace and prosperity. But, on the other hand, if we select those who are not square we simply invite fire on our own heads. This is true because in this country we have representatives of all the races and nations of the world, and any man who will not give a square deal is very likely to plunge the country into war.

In these days, among office-seekers, we generally have a class of men who declare themselves to be the best in the country, but we should study them and their record, for it is only natural that they should make professions like these, in order to win votes and be elected to office. But it is the duty of the voter to elect men whom they believe to be honest and who will "rule with righteousness." If the voters would exercise caution in these matters and elect the right kind of men, it would not be long before we would have the best government in all of the world.

2
THE QUESTION OF IMPROVEMENTS

When citizens are called to the poles to vote for bonds for improvements such as expense of school system, highways, and other projects in the interest of the city, or the state, often the laboring classes shrug their shoulders and refuse to vote for such measures, saying, "It will increase our taxes." But they should remember that without employment they would not be able to hold the property which they do have; that they would not have food, clothing, and other necessities which enable them to work for their living. Having their labor for sale and their living depending on their labor it would be wise for them to put forth effort and encourage every movement to make a suitable market in which to sell what they have to sell.

The man with money will hesitate to spend his money unless he can be sure of the profit, but, when bonds are issued he will invest, because he knows that he has ample security, and too, that it is to his best interest to keep the industrial wheel turning. No laboring man should refuse to vote for improvements for to do so is to stand in his own light and vote bread out of his mouth and the mouths of his wife and children. In this connection, I would emphasize that whenever capitalists desire to establish business enterprises of any kind it is to the best interest of the laboring man to vote permission and authority for the reasons given above.

3
A WARNING TO THE FARMER

It is often the case that the farmer assumes the wrong attitude toward improvements, and toward problems not immediately his, but he should consider the community of interests and the relationship between all these industries and his own, and he should remember that he will share in general prosperity and also in general adversity. The farmer may say "Well, I raise all I want to eat." And, going back a few years we find him making his clothes, knitting his socks and supplying other such things. But conditions have changed and now, the farmer must depend on others for what needs are outside of his own list of products.

By way of illustration, the farmer must go to the factory for his clothing and his shoes; to the manufacturing industries for his tools; to other sources of supply for others of the things he needs for his comfort and for the success of his own work; therefore he is not and can not be independent of the city and of other lines of industry, as they must depend on him for their food, for this reason there should be no antagonisms between the farmer and his city brother and fellow-laborer.

Having mutual interests they should have mutual agreements and work in harmony. So, when it comes to voting on a proposition for the benefit of the industrial workers, the farmer should readily give his support, in the interest of the whole people and not refuse because it does not concern his immediate interests, and whenever he does this he is caring for his own interests, since he is a part of the great masses and what benefits all will surely benefit him, also. In fact, while we have different groups who have their special interests, and it is well for them to safe-guard their personal and aggregate interests, strictly class legislation is wrong, selfish and disastrous.

4
LAW ENFORCEMENT

If our citizens could understand law, what is its purpose, and then would obey and enforce the law according to its purpose, we would have the best country on the globe; but there are mistakes and misunderstandings both in the keeping of the laws and in its enforcement; therefore often some of the best people are compelled to suffer unnecessarily. When a law is placed on the statute books it is supposed to protect and benefit the people and not to injure them, but, since so many of our people do not understand them, and thus suffer injury, it would be better that many of our laws were "null and void."

Of course there will be thousands who will disagree with these sentiments, but it is the opinion of the writer that it is the spirit of the law that counts rather than the letter; and that no man ought to be elected to office who will insist on enforcing the letter of the law in every particular, just because it is written on the books. A reasonable view would be that if a man is breaking the letter of the law, and yet is doing nobody any harm, he should not be molested, for to do so will do more harm than good.

Perhaps the gravest phase of law-enforcement before the American people is in connection with the 18th Amendment to the American Constitution, and in connection with which there is so much lawlessness and so much blood-shed in the name of the law. Having discussed prohibition in another place, in this connection will be found only some comments on the enforcement of this law which has not been accepted in good faith by the citizens of this nation and the writer is one of the citizens which do not approve it.

It should be recognized and fully understood that an officer of the law is not sent out to kill men, but it is his duty to arrest them and take them before the judge whose business it is to decide their fate; but, in regard to this law, as had not been true of any other efforts at enforcement, it seems that officers of the law feel it their duty to shoot men down with no excuse and giving them no opportunity for their lives. This is contrary to the spirit of the law and to the Constitution of the United States; and it is an abridgement of human rights.

When a man is employed to protect citizens and enforce the law he has no right to abuse the citizen whom he is employed to protect, for if so, he is injuring the very person whose vote gave him authority to exercise the duties of his office. An officer of this kind should be removed from office and the citizens should be wise enough never to give him such authority again. No man should trample the spirit of the law while he is zealously keeping the letter of the law.

Another thing to be considered is that one law is no more sacred than another; that all laws should be enforced, if one is; that it is rank hypocrisy to make so much fuss over one law and be so quiet when other laws are being broken openly. This, of course, has reference to the War Amendments, the 13th, 14th, and 15th Amendments to the Constitution. They were originated, passed and became a part of the Constitution just in the same way as the 18th Amendment did, yet they are violated and trampled right at the Capital of the nation and elsewhere. Just as provision was made to enforce the 18th Amendment such provision was made to enforce the other Amendments. But, in the halls of Congress men stand and mock the others and boast that they do not keep them. In this the Government is manifestly inconsistent and unjust.

5
CRIME

It is now deemed necessary to give a little time to the discussion of that mysterious thing called a crime, a thing little understood; a composite thing into which so many other things enter. The master minds of the world have given serious and earnest consideration to this question, yet none have been able to solve the problem, to accurately define crime, give its causes and the proper remedy, tho many, many remedies have been given. The study of criminology involves cause of crime; ancestral or hereditary influences; circumstances, generally spoken of as environment, apprehension and conviction of crime; and the whole punitive system by which violators of the law are punished for these crimes.

One of the most difficult phases in the consideration of crime is that which has to do with equality and justice in conviction and punishment. It is generally known that those who administer the law are inclined to be partial. There is class distinction which is unfair and unjust. In one section of the country the race problem enters in and to a large extent those of one race are punished severely for offenses which would be lightly considered if committed by members of the more prominent race. In every section of the country the rich are favored, because they can secure the best legal talent to defend them, and because they have the means with which to bribe judges and juries — and witnesses.

The discrimination in the consideration and the punishment of crime has been a source of encouragement to people to go on and do whatever they choose to do. Those who are rich think their money will exempt them from punishment; and those who are poor, and who know what is done by the upper classes, act on the theory that they are no more criminal that those of the upper classes of society who commit the same crimes, but in a different way. But the man who takes advantage of his fellow-man and commits crime against him and against society, because the immediate victim is poor, is unworthy the name man and unworthy the honor and privileges of American citizenship. Moreover, such violators cannot escape the ultimate punishment; and if they should, they are heaping up trouble for their children and the deeds of the fathers will be as millstones around the necks of their children, for generations to come. This unjust, lawless spirit is responsible for the destructive wars with their lamentable results upon human progress.

We hear much talk of sin and of crime, but these two are very closely connected. Sin is a violation of the law — especially the law of God. Crime is a violation of the laws of men. Where these human laws are in harmony with the laws of God, it is a sin to commit crime by violating the human laws. But where the laws are unjust, unfair, oppressive, and against the spirit of the law of God there may be crime in violating them, but no sin. Yet, if men will avoid sin they will avoid crime, because they are so closely connected, the one with the other.

In many instances those who make the laws are unjust in principle and violate the laws of justice by passing their unjust laws and trying to enforce them. Some of these laws tend toward crime more than toward the care of the crime; and any man or set of men who will pass such laws as are against justice or that are apt to increase crime are themselves worse that those who violate the laws. All these questions are involved in the study of crime — and they must be considered and given full weight in arriving at the facts in regard to guilt or innocence.

It is a sad fact, that in this country especially, there is a startling degree of juvenile crime; that the large majority of the criminals are youthful; that the prisons are full of young people who have committed crime; and there are underlying causes which if understood would help in the understanding of these problems and in dealing wisely and justly with them. Among the most detrimental causes must be enumerated the mistakes of parents — of both fathers and mothers, who are derelict in their own duties toward their families and thus hinder their own children.

Hereditary influence has to do with the character of the father and mother, as that character is resultant from conduct of their parents. Next in the catalogue is pre-natal influence, having to do with the conduct of the mother during the period of gestation — the period between conception and birth. Then follow environment or surroundings. Especially effective is this matter of environment, for the life of the child is affected by everything it sees, hears, or comes in contact with; and for these things which make up environment the parents are most responsible. The character of a child's environment will largely determine its course in life, and whether it shall be law-abiding or a violator of the law — a criminal.

For instance, if the parents tell lies to the children, or tell lies in the presence of the children they need not hope that theirs will be truthful children. The example of parents will be more effective in influencing the lives of their children that will their words. The children are watching and listening and it is reasonable that they should think what their parents do must be right, for those parents, to them, are the examples of all that is worthwhile in life. Especially is this true of mothers who have largely the training of the children. In this age it has been established that it is not well to do a great deal of whipping, but a mother ought to be able to use tact and manage to direct the life of her child.

Another phase of crime is what might be called "mass crime." By this is meant the criminal actions of people who form mobs and become outlaws themselves, in their determination to punish some crime committed or alleged to have been committed by some individual. In effort to punish one criminal, a hundred will commit a crime more cruel and more atrocious than the one they would punish. When this condition prevails, thousands become criminal in mind and in heart by hating the offender, or the accused, and deciding in their own minds that he should die; willing that he should die some awful death. And often expectant mothers are influenced by such a wild, lawless sinful spirit, and they thus influence their children in lawlessness even before the children are born. This means increase in crime, and such is responsible for much of the crime of today.

If crime is committed, the law ought to be allowed to take its course; the proper authorities ought to examine into the case and if the individual is guilty he ought to be punished according to the law, in the interest of human society. Then, if a man has become a habitual criminal so that he loses control of himself and becomes a menace to society, he ought to be placed somewhere in confinement so that he cannot do harm to others; but all of this should be by legally constituted authority — and all should be impartial, with no thought or consideration of race, or class, entering into consideration.

We find in the world the spirit of good and the spirit of evil, as has been true of every age; these two spirits are ever struggling for control of the lives of men; individually we are not responsible for the inclinations within us as influenced by these two spirits; but it becomes man's duty to give the good spirit chance to control. As the muddy water of the river will get clear, after a long time, so will this stream of evil become clear and the good spirit will win control; but it will take a long time, as it will take a long time for the river to become clear.

Consideration of the operations of electricity will shed light on this difficult subject of these two spirits, and will help us to understand the hold that the evil spirit has on the world today. When more force is needed, or a stronger current, they add to the "horse-power" of the machine or add more units called watts and more candle-power to the current or the instrument conducting or generating the current. Doing this we get more speed, or more power to move objects; and in light, we get more of illumination. So to intensify and encourage the spirit of evil, or the spirit of good will mean to help that one or the other to gain greater control over man.

In the matter of punishment for crime, there are two views which are prominent, especially as this refers to murder. One is in favor of what is called "capital punishment," according to the old Babylonian law of "an eye for an eye, and a tooth for a tooth." The other view is opposed to capital punishment and rather contends that it is better to punish a man for crime, but that the punishment should be by confinement in prison. The most advanced view of this imprisonment for crime is that during the time of confinement, influences should be brought to bear to enlighten the individual thus confined, improve his life, give him new ideas and new ideals and finally to send him forth from prison not an enemy to society, hating society, bent on taking revenge by committing other crimes, but penitent and determined to live a better life.

The old law of retaliation is dead; those who wrote it are dead; but Jesus and His Gospel by which men are influenced to deal generously and mercifully with those who make mistakes are very much alive; and this system of Jesus will bring peace and harmony and salvation to the world, rather than the other system. We are living in a perilous age; while there are many improvements, inventions, accomplishments, of which we have the right to be proud, yet in other ways this is the most dangerous age in the history of the world; and the criminal situation is the thing of chiefest concern in this country.

One of the most serious things in regard to these matters under discussion is that so many persons believe they are right when they are wrong, and tho wrong, they try to force other people to believe and accept their views; and often their views are wrong and the masses of the people right. One of those persons is Mr. Volstead, the author of the Volstead Law to enforce the requirements of the 18th Amendment to the National Constitution. As an instance of this mistaken judgment, I cite Mr. Volstead, author of the Volstead Law, the law by which the

Prohibition Amendment is supposed to be enforced.

No doubt Mr. Volstead is sincere in convictions; that he was trying to make peace in this country; for surely no man with common sense and any degree of intelligence would intentionally cause as much trouble and death in the country as Mr. Volstead has caused, and it seems reasonable to say that Mr. Volstead himself is more responsible for crime than any man of this age, notwithstanding that, he thought he was doing good for the people. This law has resulted in the killing of men and of defenseless women and children; in making orphans of children whose parents have been killed; and there is no way to measure the crime and suffering caused by this law — this Amendment to the Constitution of the United States of America; and who can deny it!

It was reported that the Czar of Russia imposed a tax on the poor peasants of his country, knowing at the same time, that they could not pay it, and moreover, that he did not really need the money. Sitting on the top of a monument of twenty-three billion dollars, he demanded more money from those poor people who scarcely had food to satisfy their hunger. According to reports, if the people refused or even talked back to those whose duty it was to make this collection, they would have their bowels immediately torn out.

But the Volstead Law is even worse than this, for here, they kill the men right now. Over here the government allows one brother to feed poison to another brother; in this way men are doomed to suffer, and to die a slow death. Over here, they send out the raiding parties and they destroy property, and human life, just because one man wants to make all the others live as he thinks they ought to live. If they do not think and live as he thinks they ought to do, then his law will put them into prison and make them suffer severe penalties. My conclusion is that if any man is allowed to kill me when I have committed no crime, and when I am doing nobody any harm, I consider it as great a crime as any man can commit, even though it be committed under authority of the government.

It is said that the king of Belgium built a castle and used human skulls for its foundation. He could do this because he owned the Central Congo States by right of the sword, tho he had no real or justifiable rights. According to the story, he levied on the people taxes which he knew they could not pay, and then he sent the most cruel soldiers he had to collect this tax. When the chief of a tribe was ordered into the presence of the soldiers to show cause for failure of the tribe to pay this tax, he was not even allowed to explain the situation but would be put to death and his skull sent to the King to be used in the building of his castle. The castle was built, but, like the blood of Abel that cried to God from the ground, the blood of those whose skulls were there must have cried for vengeance.

Of course there is no way to prove it, and there are those who will give no weight to the theory, but it seems reasonable to conclude that God had something to do with the punishment of Belgium. The Kaiser of the Germans got it into his mind that he could conquer the world; he undertook it with the greatest army the world had ever seen; and the castle of Belgium was one of the first to be torn down; and Belgium suffered beyond all language to describe, in the terrible World's War.

Now, I would compare this castle of righteousness Mr. Volstead would build to the castle of the King of Belgium. It is being built on the foundation of grief; the walls are human bones; it will be covered with a mantle of sorrow; it will be wrapped in human tears; and the walls will be cemented with human blood; but, like the ancient tower of Babel, it is certain to fall. I would add that any one who would pass a law that will cause the taking of life as the 18th Amendment does, and would cause men to be killed because they do not live as he thinks they should, is himself a master criminal.

Spain has one of the oldest governments in the world, and prospered in the years long gone, because it had been trained as an ally of Rome, in many things pertaining to government and to knowledge. History records the dealings of Spain with the natives of South America. Having discovered precious minerals in the earth and willing to profit by the labors of others, Spain whipped and lashed the poor helpless, ignorant natives until the population was reduced fifty percent. Now, when you compare the population of the United States and the population of South America, under those conditions, it will be seen that, for the time and under the circumstances the 18th Amendment has proved more destructive to human life than the cruelty of Spain in South America. Under the conditions one can but feel sorry for the people who are responsible for these conditions, and these crimes committed in the name of the law. Especially is this sympathy due to Mr. Volstead whose law is so much responsible for those who have been killed by officers of the law, those who have died from drinking poisoned whiskey, and the sufferings of the families of those who have been deprived of their supporters.

Now the writer has expressed his views on crime, knowing well that there will be thousands who will not agree with him. He is fully aware that these views will bring criticism; but he is certain of two things: First, he knows that he is not alone in this respect, and if he is mistaken he has the company of many of the most thoughtful individuals of the nation and of the world. Then, he knows that in differing from others and in presenting these views he is clearly within his rights guaranteed by the Declaration of Independence, the Constitution of the United States, and other statutes which set forth the "inalienable rights" of citizens and of men. Because of these convictions he makes no excuse and no apology for what he has herein expressed in regard to crime, cause, responsibility, and remedy.

V
RACE VARIETIES AND ANTAGONISMS

All who will take an unbiased look back thru the history of past events will understand, in a measure, the facts on which the members of the "Coe Colony" based their conclusions as to race origin and to race relations. They will also understand why these people considered themselves a part of the great human family; and in their estimation of themselves, think not of white or black, but common humanity and of legitimate rights and privileges as members of the one great human family. For this reason,

>   1
>   We'll look back through history's pages,
>   Down the vista of the ages,
>   Looking thus that we may find,
>   Progress of the human mind.
>
>   2
>   Looking back through Nature's gloom,
>   Forward toward its fullest bloom,
>   More and more, each day, are we
>   Baffled by Her mystery.
>
>   3
>   Reason tells 'twould not be wise
>   Any creature to despise,
>   'Cause he's of another hue,
>   As some foolishly would do.

4
Tho to many regions strayed,
Of one blood all men are made;
So no one should hate another,
Since each is to each a brother.

1
THE RECORD

As we turn back the pages of history we find Moses, the great Jewish historian, one of the greatest men of ancient times, standing out as one of the brightest stars of his race and his day, and his record is an unbiased one. So, in trading the origin of races we shall make no mistake in following the records of Moses, which record is accepted by the best scholars of all ages.

Turning to the records of Moses you will read the 30th Chapter of Genesis, where Jacob, according to this knowledge and by use of the laws of nature changed the color of the cattle of his father-in-law. According to the record, this man Jacob was the third great character of the Jewish race and was a part of God's plan, and the question is, "Who could excel him?" The lesson we get from the events in the life of Jacob is that no man can originate and perfect his own righteousness but, if he is to prosper and to have divine approval, he must submit to God's plan and allow Him to use him in His own way. If he will do this, in order to use him, God will reveal mysteries to him as he did to Jacob in this matter of changing the color of animals.

An incident of my childhood experience gave me a suggestion as to influence of conditions and circumstances on life — vegetable life and animal life. My father had a splendid fence around our yard, and I conceived the idea of having peach trees in each corner of the yard.

I was a great lover of peaches and since I believed in trying to produce what you desired, in this way, I decided to plant a peach tree in each one of these corners — and so I did. But I was surprised to find that the trees in three corners flourished while the one in the fourth corner was very slow in its development. I was determined to succeed, so I decided to investigate and find the secret of this failure on the part of the tree in the southwest corner of the yard, and, if possible, to remedy the condition and make that tree flourish as did the other trees which had been planted at the same time. But, for two years this tree failed.

One thing that encouraged me in this effort was the fact that I had saved an apple tree that seemed to be dying, and was of the opinion that I could save the peach tree, too. Now, this apple tree grew well and was very hopeful, but it began to fail; the leaves turned yellow and it seemed as if it would die. Near this tree was a pile of ashes, and tho I was ignorant, there came to my mind the thought to put some of the ashes on the roots of this tree. This I did, digging down so as to put the ashes on the very roots. After the first hard rain the tree began to improve, and from that time it continued and became a very fruitful tree.

Because of success with this apple tree, I concluded that if we are trying to do good, by some means the information will come to us for the work in hand. Now, this tree had been planted where for a number of years there had been an ash-hopper used to make lye. To the people of this day, perhaps little is known of the ash-hopper and the making of lye for use in preparing soap. The hopper was made as a general thing, by taking a barrel, knocking the heads out, and filling it with ashes. The barrel was then placed on a slanting platform, filled with ashes, and water was poured on the ashes and dripping thru, it came out lye, at the other end.

After a while, the ashes would lose strength; the lye would be exhausted, and then the ashes would be thrown away and fresh ashes used to fill the hopper. The discarded ashes would be cast on the ground near by and left there as useless. By this process this southwest corner of the yard had been covered over with ashes to quite a depth and it was this very place I had planted by peach tree that failed for two years and gave me so much concern, and caused me to fear that my tree would die and my work would be all in vain. In the meanwhile the other trees were doing well.

But a strange thing happened. The third year this tree seemed to take on new life; it had abundance of beautiful leaves, and finally it bore the finest peaches of any other trees, and the fruit on this tree was of varied colors and different flavor from that on any of the other trees. I solved the problem, for it was the chemical action of the ashes that had wrought this miracle, giving to the fruit the different colors and the different flavor. My conclusion was that throughout all nature, differences in color and in other elements are caused by influence of certain circumstances and conditions, known as environment; and that this relates to vegetation, and to all animal life, including beasts and men.

Now, we will return to Moses, the man who was loved by God and to whom God revealed many things which He did not reveal to others. Moses in his record tells that God made man of clay, and that is evident to us today, and we recognize the fact that we all are made of clay, because our bodies are built up from the vegetation which grows in the earth. Perhaps it would raise the question as to the color of the clay from which Adam was made, since there are different colors of clay, but common sense would tell us that is folly to give attention to a thing of such small importance, when there are so many other things which demand attention and which are more important. If we take the record, Genesis, we read, "In the sweat of thy face shalt thou eat bread, till thou return unto the ground; for out of it was thou taken; for dust thou art and unto dust shalt thou return."

Let it be remembered that dust comes from every part of the earth, when it is dry, and that it had no power to decide its color; that the God who made men makes no distinction as to color; that alliance and association will result in assimilation; and this will help you to understand the theories being developed in this argument. It is generally conceded that Adam, the first man was red, but that does not matter, in this discussion, for I am trying to expose the folly of certain men who attempt to divide the human race according to their prejudices rather than according to facts which we find on record.

Parting the veil and looking back to antiquity we reach the cradle of man, and the reasonable theory is that he was neither white nor black, at first. The facts are, the first family or tribe had trouble, and as is true when families have trouble, in these modern times, they began to scatter abroad, and settle in different countries. In this way they were separated from one another; and by means of their search for food, a wider separation took place. Thus man became lost from one another.

Under these conditions, those who traveled North had a very hard time to live, because there was no vegetation, and in the region of almost endless snow and bitter winds it was the test of man's wisdom and strength to keep alive, amid these circumstances. Killing other animals, using their flesh for food and their skins for clothing he learned how to preserve his life under these conditions, but it required long years and entailed much suffering for him to learn the lesson of preservation of his life, there. During these long years, by means of climatic conditions and influences, nature was changing these people, their physical characteristics and creating a new type; in a measure, making a new race. Perhaps if we could have seen these people when they went into this far north country, and then could have seen them when they came out, we might better understand this mystery. But, if we do not know the color when they went in, we do know the color when they came out.

While the chemicals of the earth might not have had anything to do with these changes, when we think of Jacob and how he caused the change in the color of the cattle, and consider the effect of the ashes on the apple tree and the peach tree, in the illustrations used, we are compelled to stop and wonder. One is inclined to ask, "Well, what has that to do with a man's color?" But, since man is an animal, and animal life comes from a germ, why could not man's color be changed as well as the color of the lower animals?

To follow this illustration, if Jacob worked these changes by putting colored poles in the water at the time of the conception by the young animals, why could not the snow-covered mountains have influence on the young mothers of the higher animals under the same circumstances. This harmonizes with the theory that climatic conditions had to do with color, and that this looking constantly at the ice and snow had influence, also; but it is known, however that the generations grew whiter as the years passed by. In regard to the straight hair, it is reasonable to conclude that keeping a close-fitting cap on the head, as must have been done to keep the head warm, would have the tendency to force the hair to grow straight — it could hardly grow otherwise. For further consideration in this matter of the hereditary influence of the color of the skin, the reader is advised to read the story found in II Kings, 5th chapter.

Now, let us journey back to the Southland, the real "Garden of Eden;" note how those people lived; how happy they were; with no need to wrap their bodies to keep them warm; no necessity to till the soil, the only special requirements being shelter from the heat of the sun and from the rain. Now, as regards to their color, black, it should be remembered that the mean temperature was over 100 degrees; that the hot sun would turn everything black; that even when things are green, the constant looking at them would seem to change them to black. Well, the young mothers in this case had no white snows to look upon, and were compelled to look at dark objects all the time; so, as the whites grew whiter as the result of the opposite conditions why should it not be so that the black ones should grow blacker and blacker by the process under discussion?

Now, it may be asked why does the hair of the darker people curl? But we can get an idea as to the why, by sticking a hair into the fire and seeing that it will draw up. If cold will draw out the hair and make it straighter, then it is but natural that heat will draw it up and make it curly. Now, the conclusion is that as the chemicals in the ground affected the vegetables to the extent of changing their color, so would the chemicals in the air, cold and heat, account for the change in the color of the skin of men, the higher animals.

But there comes the question, "What is color, after all?" And, "Why should any one worry about the matter of color?" The thing to do is to treat a man right, wherever we may meet him, no matter what may be the color of his skin, because God is Father of all and God is creator of the chemicals by which these changes are made. Such were the theories of the Coe Colony of which so much has been written in this book, and such should be the conclusion and the endeavors of all people. The thing is not if a man is white or black, but whether he is worthy or unworthy; for white or black, he is human, just the same.

There are those who contend that nature has no aim, but, in this they forget what nature has done for man. It lifted him above the brute; it made it possible for him to stand erect and to walk on two feet instead of on all fours; gave him two hands to perform his duties with; gave him a heart and mind, as a court-room and five witnesses, known as the five senses, to bring evidence to the mind that it may sit as a parliament judging the right from the wrong.

Who can define nature or who can tell of its far-reaching forces or of its wonderful beauty? It has built its Grand Canyons, drawn out its lakes and rivers, and placed in perfect form the beautiful landscape which no artist can draw with precision. In carrying you back to man we must admit that the encyclopedia tells us that the Caucasian brain weighs from five to six ounces more than the brain of the Ethiopian, but, if that be true, what lesson do we learn? Well, there is nothing in that statement to worry over, for that is nothing unusual, as far as nature is concerned.

Facts well known to the athletic world easily explain this matter. There are few men who do not have one arm stronger than the other, simply because one arm is used more than the other, and the exercise made it stronger, which is natural. Then if greater exercise will build one part of the body more than another, and make it stronger than the other part, why will it not do so in regard to any part of the body? It is reasonable to conclude that if it is true in one case it is true in another case, in fact that it is throughout the entire mechanism of man's body.

Now, here is the application: According to our theory, while the poor man in the far North was planning how to take care of this body, how to get food and clothing and remain comfortable, he was also building his brain by this exercise, for it required brain to take care of himself and for his coming generation, for without this both would have perished. On the other hand, the man down in the tropics had not the same need for brain exercise. When hungry he could go to the trees that bore fruit the whole year around. He could pluck and eat his dinner and then lie down in the shade to sleep and rest until he got hungry again. The sunlight afforded all that was needed for heat, so that there was not need for stoves and furnaces, and this man in the tropics had little to do and little to worry about. So it is readily seen that these people did not require the same amount of brain as required by those in the frigid north.

Now, it is very generally known that nature has provided every animal with something with which to protect itself, except the misfits, and the peculiarities in the world of nature ought to satisfy the curiosity of every seeker, as nature seems inclined to satisfy all. It is an unique phenomenon, for no language can accurately define it; no tongue can describe it; no skill can measure its dimensions; for it is beyond all human comprehension.

2
ANTAGONISMS

Much has been said and written concerning the people of the darker races; some part of it is true, and much, very much of it, has been untrue — has been actual lies. Some excuse might be made for speculation and theorizing, but no allowance is due for deliberate misrepresentations as practiced by the Caucasian and in regard to his brothers of the darker hue. According to these who think themselves superior, those of the darker races represent a queer specimen of humanity, and some have even denied to these people a place in the human family. But the fact is that in this respect, they are no more manifestly different from other races than the other races are different from one another.

In few instances have misrepresentation and arrant lies been more destructive to amity, peace, and good will than in the matter under discussion. These lies have been put into the histories and taught the youth in the school room; they have been so emphasized that thousands have grown up to manhood and womanhood believing them to be true; and this attitude has had the effect of increasing prejudice and in keeping it alive where it would be almost certain to die; and it is a crime against humanity and a serious reflection on those who are of the dominant group and who profess the greatest wisdom of all the ages. And believed or denied this spirit of unfairness and untruthfulness responsible for racial strife; and for destructive wars, as well.

In discussing the variety of races or colors there comes the temptation to use a parable to illustrate the diversity and the philosophy of it. The parable is that of a beautiful garden with flowers which are beautiful and attractive, all bearing agreeable perfume and yet differing in structure and color. The owner of the garden is delighted with the flowers and takes great pride in showing them to his friends. In this garden, among these beautiful flowers there is neither confusion nor strife, for all manifest their beauty and send out their perfumes without any confusion. They are there, with the variety, but one flower is not envious nor jealous of any other flower of the garden, so all dwell there and grow and prosper, living in peace and harmony together.

Now, to make the application, the human family is the garden; the different races with their varying characteristics are the flowers that grow in this beautiful garden; the God of all the universe is the Owner of this garden; no doubt He delights in all the flowers, as all are of His own planting and His cultivation; and it must be true that He does not care more for one flower than for anther one, in His own garden. In this garden of humanity there should be peace and harmony, as in the natural garden. But, to the discredit of man, God's "masterpiece," the flowers in God's garden of humanity do not dwell together in peace and amity as do those in the natural garden. These flowers of the human family are jealous, envious, disagreeable. In their relations with one another and in their dealing with one another they have strife, and confusion, and the discredit of those who are responsible for it. How deplorable! How lamentable! And how it must grieve the Divine Owner of this flower garden!

In spite of the evidences of the unity of the human race and that the Creator is no respecter of races or individuals, there are those who scorn people who are of a different color from their own; and they oppress them as did the people of Egypt oppress the Hebrews whom they held in bondage. From this spirit of oppression come the wars which have been so destructive to humanity, and which have so greatly hindered the progress of the world. People have even taught their children to hate other children who were not of their race; and these children have been taught to fear, as well as hate. It is a crime to put hatred into the minds and hearts of children; they should be taught and encouraged to love all human beings, instead of hating them.

A few years ago there lived in Kansas City, a woman who objected to being called a Negro, or colored; she insisted that she was an Ishmaelite. This woman was criticized and ridiculed by some who said she was trying to get away from her race. Perhaps she was mistaken in her contentions and in her methods, but people have always tried to get away from unpleasantness and injustice, and to better their own condition in this way. And it is unreasonable to condemn them for these efforts. They are attending to their own affairs and looking after their own best interests, and nobody should be foolish enough to blame them for exercising their rights; and many times when people judge others to be weak-minded, the judges themselves are the weak-minded ones.

Now, as to the Ishmaelites, according to the record of Moses, these were a great people but history does not give them the credit they deserve, for the same reason that it has been unfair with other people; and that reason is prejudice — and fear. Ishmael and his mother, Hagar, were outcasts because of the jealousy and the hatred of Sarah, Abraham's wife. Ishmael was Abraham's son borne to him by Hagar, his wife's Egyptian maid, and for that reason was hated by Sarah, tho she was responsible for the conduct of her husband in his association with her maid. Because of the injustice done him, Ishmael was resentful, and to an extent cruel and revengeful, yet he was more humane than those who persecuted him.

An illustration or the character of the Ishmaelites is in the fact that a company of them saved the life of Joseph, Jacob's favorite son, when his own brothers had decided to end his life. In the history of Moses much is said of Joseph, his wisdom and his work as governor of Egypt during which time he saved Egypt and other nations from perishing during the famine, but little is found of those generous Ishmaelites who saved Joseph and made it possible for him to do the great work which made his name immortal. But, men should be given credit for their good deeds as certainly as they are condemned for evil deeds. However, the way of the world is different; and it will be different until men shall learn and practice honor, justice, equity and amity toward one another. But the mind and the heart of the world must be changed before that shall be brought to pass.

3
WHAT IS IN A NAME

Many controversies have raged around this query of the great Shakespeare who seemed to conclude that there is nothing in a name, and who makes the illustrative assertion, "A rose by any other name would smell as sweet." But this theory is not acceptable to everybody; in fact there are thousands who forcibly dissent from this conclusion. This is true concerning many other theories concerning names, and especially true as it refers to national and racial names. This question assumes greater significance especially when these names are not only used to indicate racial history and racial characteristics, but also are used in sarcasm, ridicule and contempt, as some of the names used in referring to those of us who make up the racial minority in the United States.

When Blumenback, the great German naturalist, gave names to the five races, he found no name for the people of darker races in America who were and are the products and the progenies of three distinct races. Some might argue that he could not consistently give a name to a race of people not yet born; however, these people, as a race were born, but they had not lived long enough to have a name, hence the failure to so designate them, as was done in regard to the others.

At the time when Mr. Blumenbach began his study of the human skull, about 1778, the American people had not won their freedom from English rule, and doubtless that accounts for his failure in this particular. Because he was a member of the Aryan, Semitic or

Tauranian class, and because in the 18th Century at the time of his writings and the advancement of his theories, the white people had the advantage, in every way, it should not be surprising that he should have such views and express them in the way he did.

At the cradle of the white man, we find him dwelling in the Caucasus mountains, thus it was easy for him to name this race by combining sections of each name. He took 'Caus,' leaving off mountains; then, leaving off "ain" from mountains, he used it as a suffix to "caucus," and thus he invented "Caucasian." According to history Blumenbach was educated at Jena and at the famous Gottingen, and for this reason his conclusions and his opinions are accorded great weight.

Now, this preliminary discussion is to emphasize the theory and the philosophy as well as the orthography of the new name "Croutau," used in the Chronicles of the Coe Colony, to designate these people in this country who are so greatly oppressed and persecuted. They are what they are as the result of being a mixture of three distinct races, for which the American white man is almost entirely responsible. And it should not seem unreasonable that some member of this despised group should seek to give it a new name, especially to get away from the one or ones to which such stigma have been attached. The new name invented by the writer is "Croutau," as shall be explained whether the same shall be acceptable to the people concerned or those who have used the other names with contempt.

Now, according to this same Blumenbach, the term "race" represented a specific place or color, while the matter of features also entered into the discussion and conclusions. In reemphasizing color he called the white man Caucasian; the American Indian, red man; the yellow man he designated Mongolian; the brown race, he termed Malays, and the black people, Ethiopians. In spite of this catalogue, such is the blending of the races with and within one another that often it is difficult to understand where one leaves off and another begins. And why should it be otherwise, when all have come from one common stock?

We come now to the philosophy, the derivation, orthography and the interpretation of the term "Croutau," which has been a puzzle to the readers of the Chronicles herein recorded. With this contention and these conclusions few may agree, but the writer believes he has the right to so construct; and he believes that there is sufficient grounds for his conclusion. So the theory is given for whatever it may merit, and with hope that it may shed some light on this troublesome subject.

We have in these United States fourteen different colors representing our race; and if I should say fifteen I am sure that I would not be very far wrong. We have also, almost as many names as we have colors; so I have taken letters from the different names and combined them into on composite term, giving us a new name, one which I consider preferable to any of those generally used to designate the people under discussion.

"C" and "A" combined with "U" are potent letters in the term Causian, and these also are found in the other words or names applied to us. "C" is the beginning of the first two syllables of Caucasian, while "A" is a stronger factor in each syllable. The letter "R" is used in the beginning of Red man, also to begin the syllable "roon" in both octoroon and quadroon, the terms which designate one-eighth and one-fourth of Negro blood respectively. "O" is a strong letter, too, appearing twice in quadroon, four times in octoroon, and one each in mulatto, yellow, and brown; and it is repeated in color. "U" is not insignificant for it is used in the majority of the names by which the darker people are designated, as well as in the term Caucasian.

Now, drawing toward a conclusion, we find the letters mentioned, C-R-O-U to be the first letters of the name we are working out. The letters found in the last part of the name are, in order, T-A-U. The letter "T" is a strong one in white, occupying the last place save one, in this word; it occupies the same position in mulatto. While "T" doe not have the same relative position in octoroon, still it is forceful in the second syllable of this word. Once more the strength of "A" is in evidence, as used in the term black in association with "C" a strong letter.

"U", the last letter of the name is significant, being used in Causian, representing the white race, and in quadroon and mulatto, so it is given the important position at the end of the name. So the new name is spelled C-R-O-U-T-A-U. The "ou" has the sound of "oo", the "A" before it the broad sound, with the final "U" silent; so the new is Croutau, pronounced Croo-taw.

VI
COROLLARY

Such is my faith in what is herein set forth that I wish it were possible that the whole world might read it, not because it expresses my conviction but because it is truth, and I believe that if it were accepted by the world it would make a large contribution toward peace and goodwill among men. What has been written concerning Truth, Spirit, Faith, Love, Civil Government, and Race Relations, I present as the sentiment of the Coe Colony, of Pea Ridge, Kentucky. These sentiments I am presenting as I learned them from the teachings and the example of these people who, though handicapped by lack of advantages and the opposition of the dominant group, developed and practiced a system of Ethics unsurpassed by any of their generation.

It is admitted that there were some weak ones among them; that quite a number of those of the "younger generation" departed from their teachings; that now and then some one of the Colony transcended the bounds of justice; but, after all, the marvel is that they did as well as they did, under the circumstances. If the true history might be published to the world, all civilized people would wonder and would applaud the stalwart, rugged, exemplary character and the meritorious conduct of these people, as a whole, making allowances for human weaknesses as must be done in regard to all individuals and aggregations of individuals. Placing their virtues and their vices in the scales, there is no doubt but that the world would judge the virtues to vastly outweigh the vices; the strong points to more than balance the weak ones; and the verdict would be a compliment to the Coe Colony.

The writer believes that the following summary of principles is such as were the sentiments of these people, and such as would have been signed and subscribed to by Ezekiel Coe, Bill Coe, Old John Coe, Patsy Ann Coe, Mandy Coe, Mary Wilburn, and fully nine-tenths of the "Coe Colony", for ever those who were weak were but influenced by their circumstances and misconceptions of what was right, and what was just. Here is the creed they would have signed:

> I. I believe in God as the creator of all things and all men, and the Governor of the Universe.
>
> II. I believe in Jesus Christ as the Savior of the World.
>
> III. I believe in the Holy Spirit as the one unfailing guide for men in their efforts to do right and live right.
>
> IV. I believe in the brotherhood of man; that all are from one common stock; and that the matters of color and racial characteristics are not fundamental but purely circumstantial and inconsequential.
>
> V. I believe in "The Rights of Man", with the following interpretation:

1. That all men are created free.

2. That in matters of "life, liberty, the pursuit of happiness," the ownership of property and the exercise of elective franchise all should be on equality.

3. That "equality before the law", is indeed an "inalienable right," and should be accorded to all.

4. That "a man's home is his castle," and that he has the right even to take life in defense of his life and of his home.

5. That all discriminations against individuals or aggregations of individuals, on account of race or color or unfortunate circumstances are crimes against humanity.

6. That all citizens should be law abiding and law-supporting, and that punishment for crime is necessary in the interest of society; but that the law should be administered to all in the same spirit and to the same extent.

7. That in order to have an honest government the voters should select and elect to office individuals of good character and reputation, and should do this without thought of personal interests or for any possible financial consideration.

VI. I believe that the home is the foundation of the nation, and that if the nation is to be preserved it's citizens must be trained and prepared in the home.

These are the conclusions and this is the creed in which are expressed the sentiments of the people with whom this story deals, as codified and propagated by one of the loyal descendants, Samuel S. Coe, in the "Chronicles of the Coe Colony," in the year of our Lord, 1930.

FINIS

www.ingramcontent.com/pod-product-compliance
Ingram Content Group UK Ltd.
Pitfield, Milton Keynes, MK11 3LW, UK
UKHW041429180426
11947UKWH00007B/358